How To Write
BETTER BUSINESS LETTERS

Andrea B. Geffner

Department Head
English and Speech
Taylor Business Institute, N.Y.

Barron's Educational Series, Inc.
New York • London • Toronto • Sydney

© Copyright 1982 by Barron's Educational Series, Inc.

Excerpted in part from *Business English: How to Make Your Writing Work for You* by Andrea B. Geffner

All rights reserved.
No part of this book may be reproduced
in any form, by photostat, microfilm, xerography,
or any other means, or incorporated into any
information retrieval system, electronic or
mechanical, without the written permission
of the copyright owner.

All inquiries should be addressed to:
Barron's Educational Series, Inc.
250 Wireless Boulevard
Hauppauge, New York 11788

Library of Congress Catalog Card No. 81-20660
International Standard Book No. 0-8120-2509-1

Library of Congress Cataloging in Publication Data

Geffner, Andrea B.
    How to write better business letters.

    Includes index.
    1. Commercial correspondence.   I. Title.
HF5721.G43   808′.066651021   81-20660
ISBN 0-8120-2509-1   AACR2

89   620   17 16 15 14 13 12

PRINTED IN THE UNITED STATES OF AMERICA

CONTENTS

TABLE OF
MODEL LETTERS

INTRODUCTION

More and more, such phrases as "Proofreading skills" and "Ability to draft correspondence" are turning up in classified ads. Positions from clerk/typists to top-level executives require not only English fluency and a basic grounding in grammar, but an ability to convey information and ideas in clear, comprehensible language. And, unfortunately, this skill is becoming more and more rare in today's society.

However, the situation that has been dubbed an "American literacy crisis" has resulted in a large demand for individuals who can write. While jobs for skilled secretaries abound, the secretary who can do her own correspondence commands a higher salary. Some corporations have even created a new position—a literate person who can rewrite everyone else's letters.

But while the ability to compose business correspondence is a rare marketable skill, it is not an unattainable one. Despite the forbidding mystique around the act (and word) of "writing," it is not a skill one is born with. People *learn* how to write, just as they learn how to read, to type, and to operate computers. But, just like learning to type, learning to write takes work and practice. One gets better at it the more one writes.

So, given the fact that you can learn to write and then market your writing skill, this book will serve as your guide. Like any good guide, it is intended to reduce your trepidation as you enter unknown territory. It will help you get started on the right word and maintain an appropriate attitude. It will point out the *do*'s and *don't*'s within each region of business writing. And, it is hoped, it will leave you on your own, a more confident, competent writer than when you first began.

1.
BUSINESS STYLE

Tone

Second to grammatical correctness, achieving an appropriate business style may be the biggest problem for the writer of business letters. A sure sign of an inexperienced writer, in fact, is the obvious attempt to sound overly "businesslike."

> As per your request, please find enclosed herewith a check in the amount of $16.49.

Such expressions as "herewith" and "as per" contribute nothing to the message while making the letter sound stilted and stiff.

The first step, then, to writing successful business correspondence is to relax. While business letters will vary in tone from familiar to formal, they should all sound natural. Within the limits of standard English, of course, you should try to say things in a "regular" way:

> As you requested, I am enclosing a check for $16.49.

If you resist the temptation to sound businesslike, you will end up being more business-minded. The second version of our sample sentence is not only more personal and friendly; it is also more efficient. It uses fewer words, taking less time to write and type as well as to read and comprehend.

With this initial piece of advice in mind, review the following list of words and expressions. Then plan to eliminate these terms from your business writing vocabulary.

EXPRESSIONS TO AVOID IN BUSINESS LETTERS

according to our records
acknowledge receipt of
as to, with reference to,
  with regard to, with
  respect to
at hand, on hand
attached please find,
  attached hereto, enclosed
  herewith, enclosed please
  find
beg to inform, beg to tell
duly
for your information
hereby, heretofore, herewith

I have your letter
I wish to thank, may I ask
in due time, in due course of
  time
in receipt of
in the near future
in view of
our Mrs. Campbell
permit me to say
pursuant to
thank you again
thank you in advance
thereon

Instead of . . .	*Use . . .*
advise, inform	say, tell, let us know
along these lines, on the order of	like, similar to
as per	as, according to
at an early date, at your earliest convenience	soon, today, next week, *a specific date*
at this time, at the present time, at this writing	now, at present
check to cover	check for
deem	believe, consider
due to the fact that, because of the fact that	because
favor, communication	letter, memo, *et al*
for the purpose of	for
forward	send
free of charge	free
in accordance with	according to
in advance of, prior to	before
in compliance with	as you requested
in re, re	regarding, concerning
in the amount of	for
in the event that	if, in case
kindly	please
of recent date	recent
party	person, *a specific name*
said	*not to be used as an adjective*
same	*not to be used as a noun*
subsequent to	after, since
the writer, the undersigned	I/me
up to this writing	until now

Consider the difference between these two versions of the same letter:

Dear Mr. Pendleton:

With reference to your order for a Nashito 35 mm camera, we are in receipt of your check and are returning same.

I beg to inform you that, as a manufacturer, our company sells cameras to dealers only. In compliance with our wholesale agreements, we deem it best to refrain from direct business with private consumers.

For your information, there are many retailers in your vicinity who carry Nashito cameras. Attached please find a list of said dealers.

Hoping you understand.

Yours truly,

- -

Dear Mr. Pendleton:

We have received your order for a Nashito 35 mm camera but, unfortunately, must return your check.

As a manufacturer, we sell cameras only to dealers, with whom we have very explicit wholesale agreements.

Nevertheless, we sincerely appreciate your interest in Nashito products. We are therefore enclosing a list of retailers in your community who carry a full line of our cameras. Any one of them will be happy to serve you.

Sincerely yours,

Outlook

While striving for a natural tone, you should also aim for a positive outlook. Even when the subject of your letter is unpleasant, it is important to remain courteous and tactful. Building and sustaining the goodwill of your reader should be an underlying goal of nearly any letter you write. Even a delinquent account may someday become a paying customer.

A simple "please" or "thank you" is often enough to make a mundane letter more courteous. Instead of:

> We have received your order.

you might try:

> Thank you for your recent order.

Or, in place of the impersonal:

> Checking our records, we have verified the error in your November bill.

you could help retain a customer by writing:

> Please accept our sincere apologies for the error in your November bill.

Saying "We are sorry" or "I appreciate" can do much to build rewarding business relations.

On the other hand, you must be tactful when delivering unpleasant messages. NEVER accuse your reader with expressions like "your error" or "your failure." An antagonistic letter would say:

> Because you have refused to pay your long overdue bill, your credit rating is in jeopardy.

A more diplomatic letter (and therefore one more apt to get results) might say:

> Because the $520 balance on your account is now over ninety days past due, your credit rating is in jeopardy.

Because the second sentence refrains from attacking the reader personally (and also includes important details), it will be read more openly.

A word of caution is necessary here. Some writers, in an effort to be pleasant, end their letters with sentence fragments:

Looking forward to your early reply.
Hoping to hear from you soon.
Thanking you for your interest.

These participial phrases (note the -ING form in each) should NOT be used to conclude a letter. There is never an excuse for grammatical flaws, especially when complete sentences will serve the purpose well:

We look forward to your early reply.
I hope to hear from you soon.
Thank you for your interest.

Consider the difference between these two versions of the same memo:

TO: Department Supervisors

FROM: Assistant Director

Inform your subordinates:

1 Because so many have taken advantage of past leniency, lateness will no longer be overlooked. Paychecks will be docked as of Monday, March 6.

2 As a result of abuses of employee privileges, which have resulted in exorbitant long distance telephone bills, any employee caught making a personal call will be subject to disciplinary action.

As supervisors, you will be required to enforce these new regulations.

- -

TO: _____

FROM: Wanda Hatch, Assistant Director

Unfortunately, a few people have taken advantage of lenient company policies regarding lateness and personal phone calls. As a result, we must all now conform to tougher regulations.

Please inform the members of your department that:

1 Beginning Monday, March 6, the paychecks of employees who are late will be docked.

2 Personal phone calls are no longer permitted.

It is a shame that the abuses of a few must cost the rest of us. But we are asking all department supervisors to help us enforce these new rules.

- -

The "You Approach"

Courtesy and tact are sometimes achieved by what is called a *"you ap-proach."* That is, your letter should be reader oriented and sound as if you share your reader's point of view. For example:

> Please accept our apologies for the delay.

is perfectly polite. But:

> We hope you have not been seriously inconvenienced by the delay.

lets your reader know that you care.

This, of course, does NOT mean you should avoid "I" and "we" when necessary. When you do use these pronouns, though, keep a few pointers in mind:

1. Use "I" when you are referring to yourself (or to the person who will actually sign the letter).
2. Use "we" when you are referring to the company itself.
3. DO NOT use the company name or "our company," both of which, like the terms listed earlier in this chapter, sound stilted. This practice is rather like referring to oneself by one's name, rather than "I" or "me."

Also, you should be careful to use your reader's name sparingly in the body of your letter. Although this practice seems, at first glance, to personalize a letter, it can sound condescending.

Now, compare the two letters that follow, and see if you recognize the features that make the second letter more *"you*-oriented."

Dear Ms. Biggs:

Having conducted our standard credit investigation, we have concluded that it would be unwise for us to grant you credit at this time.

We believe that the extent of your current obligations makes you a bad credit risk. As you can understand, it is in our best interest to grant charge accounts only to those customers with proven ability to pay.

Please accept our sincere regrets and feel free to continue to shop at Allen's on a cash basis.

Sincerely yours,

- -

Dear Ms. Biggs:

I am sorry to inform you that your application for an Allen's charge account has been turned down.

Our credit department believes that, because of your current obligations, additional credit might be difficult for you to handle at this time. Your credit reputation is too valuable to be placed in jeopardy.

We will be delighted, of course, to reconsider your application in the future should your financial responsibilities be reduced. Until then, we hope you will continue to shop at Allen's where EVERY customer is our prime concern.

Sincerely yours,

- -

Organization

One last word about style: a good business letter must be well organized. You must *plan in advance* everything you want to say; you must *say everything necessary* to your message; and then you must stop. That is, a letter must be logical, complete, and concise.

When planning a letter and before you start to write, jot down the main point you want to make. Then, list all the details necessary to make that point; these may be facts, reasons, explanations, etc. Finally, rearrange your list; in the letter, you will want to mention things in a logical order so that your message will come across as clearly as possible.

Making a letter complete takes place during the planning stage, too. Check your list to make sure you have included all the relevant details; the reader of your finished letter must have all the information he or she will need. In addition to facts, reasons, and explanations, necessary information could also entail an appeal to your reader's emotions or understanding. In other words, SAY EVERYTHING YOU CAN TO ELICIT FROM YOUR READER THE RESPONSE YOU'D LIKE.

On the other hand, you must be careful not to say too much. You must know when a letter is finished. If a message is brief, resist the temptation to "pad" it; if you've said what you have to say in just a few lines, don't try to fill the letter out. One mistake is to reiterate an idea. If you've already offered your thanks, you will upset the logical order and, therefore, the impact of your letter if you end with:

Thank you once again.

Tacking on a separate additional message will similarly weaken the effect of your main point. Imagine receiving for a long overdue bill a collection letter which concludes:

Let us take this opportunity to remind you that our January White Sales begin next week, with three preview days for our special charge customers.

Don't, moreover, give your reader more information than is needed:

Because my husband's birthday is October 12, I would like to order the three-piece luggage ensemble in your fall catalog.

Certainly, an order clerk would much prefer to know the style number of the luggage than the date of your husband's birth.

In a similar vein, you should strive to eliminate redundant words and phrases from your letters. For example:

I have received your invitation *inviting me* to participate in your annual Career Conference.

Since all invitations invite, the words *inviting me* are superfluous. Another common mistake is to say:

the green-colored carpet

or:

the carpet that is green in color

Green *is* a color, so to use the word *color* is wordy.

Adverbs are often the cause of redundancy:

> If we cooperate together, the project will be finished quickly.

Cooperate already means work together, so using the word *together* is unnecessary.

Also, when one word will accurately replace several, use the one word. Instead of:

> Mr. Kramer handled the job *in an efficient manner.*

say:

> Mr. Kramer handled the job *efficiently.*

The following list of common redundancies should help you eliminate the problem from your writing:

REDUNDANT EXPRESSIONS

Don't Use . . .	*Use . . .*
and et cetera	et cetera
as otherwise	otherwise
at about	about
attached hereto	attached
avail oneself of	use
be of the opinion	believe
both alike	alike
both together	together
check into	check
connect up	connect
continue on	continue
cooperate together	cooperate
customary practice	practice
each and every	each *or* every
enclosed herewith	enclosed
enter into	enter
forward by post	mail
have a tendency to	tend to
in many instances	often
in the amount of	for
in the matter of	about
in the process of being	being
in this day and age	nowadays
inform of the reason	tell why
letter under date of	letter of
letter with regard to	letter about
new beginner	beginner
on account of the fact that	because
past experience	experience
place emphasis on	emphasize
place an order for	order
repeat again	repeat
same identical	identical
send an answer	reply
up above	above
write your name	sign

Now consider the following two sample letters. Notice the redundancies in the first that are eliminated in the second.

Dear Ms. Rodriguez:

I am very pleased with the invitation that I received from you inviting me to make a speech for the National Association of Secretaries on June 11. Unfortunately, I regret that I cannot attend the meeting on June 11. I feel that I do not have sufficient time to prepare myself because I received your invitation on June 3 and it is not enough time to prepare myself completely for the speech.

Yours truly,

- -

Dear Ms. Rodriguez:

I am pleased with the invitation to speak to the National Association of Secretaries. Unfortunately, I cannot attend the meeting on June 11.

I feel that I will not have sufficient time to prepare myself because I received your invitation on June 3.

I will be happy to address your organization on another occasion if you would give me a bit more notice. Best of luck with your meeting.

Sincerely yours,

- -

Of course, as you exclude irrelevant details and redundancies, you should be careful NOT to cut corners by leaving out necessary words. For example, some writers, in a misguided attempt at efficiency, omit articles *(the, a,* and *an)* and prepositions:

Please send order special delivery.

The only effect of omitting "the" and "by" here—

Please send the order by special delivery.

—is to make the request curt and impersonal.

★ **PRACTICE CORRESPONDENCE**

A. In the space provided, rewrite each sentence to eliminate the stilted tone.

Example:

We are in receipt of your letter dated December 13, 1982.
We have received your letter of December 13, 1982.

1. Please advise us as to your decision.

_____

_____

2. In the event that your bill has already been paid, kindly disregard this reminder.

_____

_____

3. Due to the fact that your subscription has not been renewed, the next issue of *Run!* will be your last.

_____

_____

4. Feel free to contact the undersigned if you have any questions.

_____

_____

5. Pursuant to our telephone conversation of Friday last, I would like to verify our agreement.

_____

_____

6. Subsequent to last month's meeting, several new policies have gone into effect.

_____

_____

7. Please forward your order at your earliest convenience.

_____

_____

8. Our deluxe model copier is on the order of a Rolls Royce in terms of quality and precision.

_____

_____

9. Enclosed please find a self-addressed reply card for the purpose of your convenience.

_____

_____

10. I beg to inform you that, despite your impressive background, we feel that your skills do not quite match our needs.

_____

_____

B. In the space provided, replace each expression with one or two words that convey the same meaning.

1. type out from shorthand notes

_____

2. a shopkeeper with a good reputation

_____

3. performed the work with great effect

_____

4. a sharp rise in prices accompanied by a fall in the value of currency

_____

5. some time in the near future

_____

6. ran off several copies of the original on a duplicating machine

_____

7. people with the responsibility of managing an office

_____

8. suffering from fatigue

_____

9. in a decisive way

_____

10. handwriting that is nearly impossible to read

_____

_____

C, D, E. On another sheet of paper, rewrite these letters to make them more courteous, concise, and *you*-oriented.

Dear Ms. Lawson:

I regret to inform you that we are completely booked up for the week of August 22. We have no rooms available because the National Word Processors Association will be holding their convention at our hotel during the week of August 22. As you will surely understand, we have to reserve as many rooms as possible for members of the association.

If you can't change the date of your trip, maybe you could find the double room with bath that you want at another hotel here in Little Rock.

Cordially,

- -

Dear Mr. Ross:

With reference to your letter of Thursday last, I can't answer it because my boss, Ms. Leonard, is out of town. If I gave you any information about the new contract with Hastings Development Corporation, she might not like it.

If Ms. Leonard wants you to have that information, I'll have her write to you when she returns in two weeks.

Yours truly,

Dear Ms. Graham:

The information you want having to do with filing for an absentee ballot for the upcoming Presidential election, is not available from our office.

Why don't you write your local Board of Elections?

Sorry.

Sincerely yours,

2. LETTER FORMAT

Before we begin to discuss letter *content,* we must examine letter appearance, for it is the physical condition of a letter that makes the first impression on your reader. Before reading even one word you have written, the reader has formed an opinion based on the way your letter looks—the arrangement, the typing quality, etc.

When you have composed the body of your letter and are ready to type, keep in mind three things:

Typing Letters should be single-spaced with double spacing between paragraphs. Typing should be neat and dark. Errors should not be erased; correction fluid or paper should be used instead.

Paragraphing Paragraph breaks should come at logical points in your message and should also result in an EVEN appearance. A one-line paragraph followed by an eight-line paragraph will look bottom heavy. Paragraphs of *approximately* the same length will please the eye.

White space In addition to the space created by paragraphing, leave space by centering your letter on the page. An ample margin of white space should surround the message, top and bottom as well as both sides. If a letter is brief, avoid beginning to type too high on the page; if a letter is long, do not hesitate to use an additional sheet of paper. (See Figure 2-1 for recommended spacing between letter parts.)

Parts of a Business Letter

While the horizontal placement of letter parts may vary (see the next section, "Arrangement Styles"), the vertical order of these parts is standard. Refer to the model letter (Figure 2-1) as you study the following list of letter parts.

1) LETTERHEAD: This, of course, is printed and supplied by your employer. It is used only for the first page of a letter.

2) DATELINE: The date on which the letter is being prepared is typed a few lines below the letterhead.

3) INSIDE ADDRESS: The address of your reader is typed as it will appear on the envelope.

4) ATTENTION LINE: This is not always required. It should be used when the letter is addressed to a company or organization as a whole, but

you want it to be handled by a specific individual at the company or within the organization. It should be underlined or typed in capitals.

5) SALUTATION: While "Dear Sir," "Dear Madam," and "Gentlemen" are acceptable in cases of extreme formality, you should otherwise use an individual's name whenever it is known. When the reader's name is *not* known, the person's title is the next best term in a salutation.

6) SUBJECT LINE: Like the attention line, this is often omitted, but its inclusion is a courtesy to your reader. By alerting him to the content of your message, you enable him to decide whether the letter requires immediate attention. It should be underlined or typed in capitals.

7) BODY: This is the actual message of your letter.

8) COMPLIMENTARY CLOSING: This is a polite, formal way to end a letter; standard forms are "Yours truly" or "Truly yours," "Sincerely yours," "Respectfully yours," etc. Overly familiar closings should be avoided, except in special situations. "Best wishes," for example, could be used when the reader is well known to you. Expressions such as "Fondly" or "Love" should, obviously, be reserved for private correspondence.

9) COMPANY SIGNATURE: Another item often omitted from less formal correspondence, it should be used when the signer of the letter is writing as a spokesperson for the company, not as an individual. Since this information appears in the letterhead, some companies omit it altogether.

10) SIGNER'S IDENTIFICATION: Typed four lines below the previous item to allow space for the signature, this includes the signer's name and any relevant titles.

11) REFERENCE INITIALS: Consisting of the signer's initials in capitals followed by a slash or colon followed by the typist's lowercase initials, this item serves as a reminder of who prepared the letter.

12) ENCLOSURE REMINDER: Consisting of the word "enclosure," or "enclosure" followed by a list of the enclosed items, this is a practical courtesy to prevent your reader from discarding important matter with the envelope.

13) "CC" NOTATION: Also a courtesy, this tells the reader who has been sent a carbon copy of the letter.

FLANAGAN'S DEPARTMENT STORE
(1)
12207 Sunset Strip
Los Angeles, California 91417

(2)   June 7, 19--

Ketchum Collection Agency
(3)   1267 Hollywood Boulevard
Los Angeles, California 91401

(4)   ATTENTION: MS. TERRY ROBERTS

(5)   Gentlemen:

(6)   Subject: Mr. Gary Daniels, Account #69 112 003

We would like to turn over to your services the account of Mr. Gary Daniels, 4441 Natick Avenue, Sherman Oaks, California 91418. The balance on Mr. Daniels' account, $829.95, is now 120 days past due; and, although we have sent him four statements and five letters, we have been unable to collect his debt.

(7)   Mr. Daniels is employed by West Coast Furniture Showrooms, Inc. He banks at the Natick Avenue branch of Third National City Bank and has been a customer of ours for four years. We have enclosed his file for your reference.

We are confident that we can rely on Ketchum as we have in the past. Please let us know if there is any further information with which we can furnish you.

(8)   Sincerely yours,

(9)   FLANAGAN'S DEPARTMENT STORE

(10)   Martha Fayman
Credit Manager

(11)   MF/wg
(12)   Enclosure
(13)   cc Mr. Norman Hyman

Figure 2-1

THE PARTS OF A BUSINESS LETTER

Arrangement Styles

As previously noted, the horizontal placement of letter parts is flexible—within the limits of five basic styles. Often, however, a company will have a preferred arrangement style which employees are required to use.

FULL-BLOCKED (Figure 2-2): All letter parts begin at the left margin. It is therefore the fastest traditional arrangement style to type.

BLOCKED (Figure 2-3): Like full-blocked, all letter parts begin at the left margin, *except* the dateline, complimentary closing, company signature, and writer's identification, which start at the horizontal center of the page. (Options—the dateline may end at the right margin; attention and subject lines may be centered or indented five or ten spaces.)

SEMI-BLOCKED *or* MODIFIED BLOCKED (Figure 2-4): This is the same as a blocked letter with one change: the beginning of each paragraph is indented five or ten spaces.

SQUARE-BLOCKED (Figure 2-5): This is the same as a full-blocked letter with two changes: the date is typed on the same line as the start of the inside address and ends at the right margin; reference initials and enclosure reminder are typed on the same lines as the signature and signer's identification. As a result, corners are squared off. This arrangement saves space, allowing longer letters to be fit onto a single page. (Be sure to use a line at least 50 spaces long so that the inside address won't run into the dateline.)

SIMPLIFIED *or* AMS (Figure 2-6): Designed by the Administrative Management Society, this style uses open punctuation and is the same as full-blocked, except: (1) no salutation or complimentary closing is used; (2) an entirely capitalized subject line (without the word "subject") *must* be used; (3) the signer's identification is typed in all capitals; and (4) lists are indented five spaces unless numbered or lettered (in which case they are blocked with no periods after the numbers or letters). This style is extremely efficient, requiring much less time to type than other styles. However, it is also impersonal. For this reason, the reader's name should be mentioned at least once in the body.

Punctuation Styles

Regardless of punctuation style, the *only* letter parts (outside of the body) to be followed by punctuation marks are the salutation and complimentary closing. Within the body, the general rules of punctuation apply.

OPEN: No punctuation is used, except in the body. (See Figure 2-2.)

STANDARD: The salutation is followed by a colon; the complimentary closing is followed by a comma. (See Figure 2-3.)

Note: The salutation and closing should be punctuated consistently: either *both* are followed by punctuation or *neither* is followed by punctuation. Note, too, that a comma is NOT used after the salutation. (This practice is reserved for private correspondence.)

NATIONAL ORGANIZATION OF RETIRED PERSONS
Freeport High School
Freeport, Vermont 66622

October 14, 19--

Ms. Iva Stravinsky
Attorney-at-Law
200 Center Street
Freeport, Vermont 66621

Dear Ms. Stravinsky

Subject: Guest Lecture

The members of the Freeport chapter of the National Organization of Retired Persons would indeed be interested in a lecture on "The Social Security Act: What It Means to You." Therefore, with much appreciation, I accept your offer to address our club.

The NORP meets every Tuesday at 8 P.M. in the auditorium of Freeport High School. The programs for our meetings through November 20th have already been established. However, I will call you in a few days to schedule a date for your lecture for the first Tuesday after the 20th that meets your convenience.

The membership and I look forward to your lecture on a topic so important to us all.

Sincerely yours

NATIONAL ORGANIZATION OF RETIRED PERSONS

Henry Purcell
President

HP/bm

Figure 2-2

FULL-BLOCKED LETTER STYLE

NATIONAL ORGANIZATION OF RETIRED PERSONS
Freeport High School
Freeport, Vermont 66622

October 14, 19--

Ms. Iva Stravinsky
Attorney-at-Law
200 Center Street
Freeport, Vermont 66621

Dear Ms. Stravinsky:

Subject: Guest Lecture

The members of the Freeport chapter of the National Organization of Retired Persons would indeed be interested in a lecture on "The Social Security Act: What It Means to You." Therefore, with much appreciation, I accept your offer to address our club.

The NORP meets every Tuesday at 8 P.M. in the auditorium of Freeport High School. The programs for our meetings through November 20th have already been established. However, I will call you in a few days to schedule a date for your lecture for the first Tuesday after the 20th that meets your convenience.

The membership and I look forward to your lecture on a topic so important to us all.

Sincerely yours,

Henry Purcell
President

HP/bm

Figure 2-3
BLOCKED LETTER STYLE

NATIONAL ORGANIZATION OF RETIRED PERSONS
Freeport High School
Freeport, Vermont 66622

October 14, 19--

Ms. Iva Stravinsky
Attorney-at-Law
200 Center Street
Freeport, Vermont 66621

Dear Ms. Stravinsky:

Subject: Guest Lecture

The members of the Freeport chapter of the National Organization of Retired Persons would indeed be interested in a lecture on "The Social Security Act: What It Means to You." Therefore, with much appreciation, I accept your offer to address our club.

The NORP meets every Tuesday at 8 P.M. in the auditorium of Freeport High School. The programs for our meetings through November 20th have already been established. However, I will call you in a few days to schedule a date for your lecture for the first Tuesday after the 20th that meets your convenience.

The membership and I look forward to your lecture on a topic so important to us all.

Sincerely yours,

Henry Purcell
President

HP/bm

Figure 2-4

SEMI-BLOCKED LETTER STYLE

NATIONAL ORGANIZATION OF RETIRED PERSONS
Freeport High School
Freeport, Vermont 66622

Ms. Iva Stravinsky   October 14, 19--
Attorney-at-Law
200 Center Street
Freeport, Vermont 66621

Dear Ms. Stravinsky:

SUBJECT: GUEST LECTURE

The members of the Freeport chapter of the National Organization of
Retired Persons would indeed be interested in a lecture on "The
Social Security Act: What It Means to You." Therefore, with much
appreciation, I accept your offer to address our club.

The NORP meets every Tuesday at 8 P.M. in the auditorium of
Freeport High School. The programs for our meetings through November 20th have already been established. However, I will call you
in a few days to schedule a date for your lecture for the first Tuesday
after the 20th that meets your convenience.

The membership and I look forward to your lecture on a topic so
important to us all.

Sincerely yours,

NATIONAL ORGANIZATION OF RETIRED PERSONS

Henry Purcell
President   HP/bm

Figure 2-5

SQUARE-BLOCKED LETTER STYLE

NATIONAL ORGANIZATION OF RETIRED PERSONS
Freeport High School
Freeport, Vermont 66622

October 14, 19--

Ms. Iva Stravinsky
Attorney-at-Law
200 Center Street
Freeport, Vermont 66621

GUEST LECTURE

The members of the Freeport chapter of the National Organization of Retired Persons would indeed be interested in a lecture on "The Social Security Act: What It Means to You." Therefore, with much appreciation, I accept your offer to address our club.

The NORP meets every Tuesday at 8 P.M. in the auditorium of Freeport High School. The programs for our meetings through November 20th have already been established. However, I will call you in a few days to schedule a date for your lecture for the first Tuesday after the 20th that meets your convenience.

The membership and I look forward, Ms. Stravinsky, to your lecture on a topic so important to us all.

HENRY PURCELL, PRESIDENT

HP/bm

Figure 2-6

SIMPLIFIED LETTER STYLE

Postscripts

It is advisable to avoid postscripts; when a letter is well planned, all pertinent information will be included in the body. However, when a postscript is required, it is arranged as the other paragraphs in the letter have been, preceded by "P.S." or "PS":

> P.S.   Let me remind you of our special discount on orders for a dozen or more of the same model appliance.

Special Paragraphing

When a message contains quotations of prices or notations of special data, this information is set in a special paragraph (see Figure 2-7), indented five spaces on the left and right, preceded and followed by a blank line.

The Envelope

An envelope should be addressed to correspond with the inside address. On an envelope, though, the state name may be abbreviated in accordance with the United States Postal Service ZIP-code style. On a standard business-size envelope, the address should begin four inches from the left edge, fourteen lines from the top (see Figure 2-8).

In accordance with Postal Service guidelines, the address should be blocked and single-spaced; and it should include the ZIP code one space after the state. Because NO information should appear below the ZIP code, special instructions (such as *ATT: Mr. Smith* or *Please Forward*) should be placed four lines below the return address. Similarly, mailing services, such as *Airmail* or *Certified Mail,* should be typed below the stamp.

The return address, matching the letterhead, is usually printed on business envelopes.

FRANKLIN AND GORDON OFFICE SUPPLIES, INC.
72-01 Lefferts Boulevard
Rego Park, New York 11206

September 15, 19--

Robert Nathan, CPA
222 Bergen Street
New Orleans, Louisiana 77221

Dear Mr. Nathan:

We appreciate your interest in Franklin and Gordon office supplies and are delighted to send you the information you requested:

Ruled ledger paper, by the ream only, costs $25; with the purchase of six or more reams, the price is reduced to $22 per ream, a savings of at least $18.

Black, reinforced ledger binders are $14 each; with the purchase of six or more binders, the price is only $12 each, a savings of at least $12.

Because we are the manufacturers of many other fine office supplies, ranging from ball-point pens to promotional novelties, we have enclosed for your consideration a copy of our current catalog. Should you decide to place an order, you may use the convenient order form in the center of the catalog.

Please let us know if we may be of further assistance.

Sincerely yours,

FRANKLIN AND GORDON OFFICE SUPPLIES, INC.

George Gillian
Customer Service Manager

GG:jc
Enclosure

Figure 2-7

SPECIAL PARAGRAPHING

FLANAGAN'S DEPARTMENT STORE
12207 Sunset Strip
Los Angeles, CA 91417

Attention Ms. Terry Roberts   Registered Mail

                    Ketchum Collection Agency
                    1267 Hollywood Boulevard
                    Los Angeles, CA 91401

Figure 2-8

THE ENVELOPE

★ PRACTICE CORRESPONDENCE

Type this letter in each of the five arrangement styles: (A) Full-blocked, (B) Blocked, (C) Semi-blocked, (D) Square-blocked, and (E) Simplified.

Dateline: July 9, 19—
Inside Address: The Middle Atlantic Institute of Technology, 149 Danbury Road, Danbury, Connecticut 50202
Attention Line: Attention Dean Claude Monet
Salutation: Dear Sirs
Subject Line: Educational Exchange
Body:

The Commission for Educational Exchange between the United States and Belgium has advised me to contact you in order to obtain employment assistance.

I received my Doctor's Degree with a "grande distinction" from the University of Brussels and would like to teach French (my mother tongue), English, Dutch, or German.

My special field is English literature; I wrote my dissertation on James Joyce, but I am also qualified to teach languages to business students. I have been active in the field of applied linguistics for the past two years at the University of Brussels.

I look forward to hearing from you.
Complimentary Closing: Respectfully yours
Signer's Identification: Jacqueline Brauer
Reference Initials: JB:db

3.
REQUEST LETTERS

As a businessperson, you will inevitably have to write many request letters. The need for information or special favors, services, or products arises daily in almost every type of business. The reasons for writing a request letter are diverse:

1) to obtain information (such as prices or technical data);
2) to receive printed matter (such as booklets, catalogs, price lists, and reports);
3) to receive sample products;
4) to order merchandise;
5) to engage services (including repair or maintenance services);
6) to make reservations (at hotels, restaurants, theaters, etc.);
7) to seek special favors (such as permission, assistance, or advice).

While certain requests, such as ordering merchandise, are routine matters, the general guidelines for business letter writing are especially important when writing any request. Tact and courtesy are essential when you want your reader to *act.* And if you want him to act *promptly,* your letter must encourage him to do so. Therefore, all requests should:

1) be specific and brief;
2) be reasonable;
3) provide complete, accurate information.

Inquiries

Usually, an inquiry offers the recipient no immediate reward or advantage beyond the prospect of a future customer or the maintenance of goodwill. Therefore, your inquiry must be worded in such a way that the recipient will respond despite a hectic schedule. To do this, you must make your inquiry *easy to answer.*

First of all, you should decide exactly what you want *before* you write. This should include the specific information that you need as well as the course of action you would like your reader to take. Consider this request:

Dear Sirs:

Please send us information about your office copiers so that we will know whether one would be suited to our type of business.

Yours truly,

The recipient of this letter would be at a total loss to respond. Other than simply sending a brochure or catalog, she could not possibly explain the advantages of her company's machines without knowing your company's needs. You have *not* made it easy for her to act.

Such an inquiry should include specific questions worded to elicit specific facts. Since the manufacturer of copiers may make dozens of models, the inquiry should narrow down the type your company would consider.

Note how the revised letter (Figure 3-1) makes it easier for your reader to respond. You have given a clear picture of what you're looking for, so she can determine which of the company's products might interest you. Moreover, by mentioning the REASON for your inquiry, you motivate her re-

---

MAHONEY AND MILLMAN, INC.
1951 Benson Street
Bronx, New York 10465

May 2, 19--

RBM Manufacturing Company, Inc.
4022 Ninth Avenue
New York, New York 10055

Dear Sirs:

We intend to purchase a new office copier before the end of the fiscal year. We would like to consider an RBM copier and wonder if you have a model that would suit our needs.

Our office is small, and a copier would generally be used by only three secretaries. We run approximately 3,000 copies a month and prefer a machine that uses regular paper. We would like a collator, but rarely need to run off more than 25 copies at any one time.

We would also like to know about your warranty and repair service.

Since our fiscal year ends June 30, 19--, we hope to hear from you soon.

Sincerely yours,

William Wilson
Office Manager

WW/sw

Figure 3-1

INQUIRY

sponse. (Your intended purchase is a real potential sale for RBM.) Finally, by letting her know WHEN you intend to buy, you've encouraged her to reply promptly.

When a request does *not* hold the prospect for a potential sale, you should make your letter even more convenient for your reader:

1) Itemize and list the specific facts you want.
2) Enclose a self-addressed, stamped envelope.
3) Suggest a way in which you can reciprocate.

Dear Mr. Greenbaum:

I am taking a course in Principles of Advertising at Smithville Community College in Smithville, Ohio, and am doing my term project on the ways in which American automobile manufacturers are now competing in the small-car market.

I would therefore greatly appreciate your sending me the following specifications on the new RX-7:

1 Fuel economy statistics

2 Technological advances (such as steering system, brake system, and engine capacity)

3 Available options

I would also find it very helpful if you told me in which magazine (or other mass media) you began your advertising campaign.

I am certain my classmates will find this information extremely interesting. I will be sure to send you a copy of my report as soon as it is complete.

Respectfully yours,

Orders

Many companies use special forms for ordering merchandise or service. They may use their own, called a *purchase order,* or one provided by the seller, called an *order form.* These forms have blank spaces to insure the inclusion of all necessary information. Their advantage is that they enable a company to number and so carefully file all expenditures.

Nevertheless, there will be times when an order must be put into letter format. At such times, you must be sure to include COMPLETE, ACCURATE INFORMATION because incomplete orders result in delayed deliveries, and inaccurate facts result in receipt of the wrong merchandise.

Every order should include:

1) the name of the item being ordered;
2) the item's number (catalog number, style number, model number, etc.);
3) quantity desired (often in large units such as dozens, cases, reams, etc.);
4) description (such as size, weight, color, material, finish, extra features);
5) unit price;
6) applicable discounts;

7) applicable sales tax;

8) total price;

9) method of payment (such as charge account, including the account number; c.o.d.; check; etc.);

10) desired delivery date;

11) method of shipment (such as parcel post or air express);

12) delivery address (which may vary from the billing address);

13) authorized signature.

In addition, if your order is in response to an advertisement, you should mention the source (such as the title and issue date of a magazine or newspaper).

The following letter would run into trouble:

Dear Sirs:

Please send me one of your weather vanes which I saw advertised for $34.95. We have recently repainted our garage, and a weather vane would be a wonderful finishing touch.

My check is enclosed.

Sincerely,

First of all, an order clerk would not know what to send this customer unless the company manufactured only one style of weather vane for $34.95. Moreover, instead of providing NECESSARY FACTS, the writer included unnecessary details. Generally, IT IS NOT NECESSARY TO MENTION A REASON FOR AN ORDER. Orders are routine and handled in quantity; as long as you are a paying customer, your impetus for buying does not interest the seller.

While the preceding letter would require interim correspondence before the order could be shipped, the letter in Figure 3-2 would elicit prompt delivery.

250 Commonwealth Avenue
Boston, Massachusetts 02118
February 14, 19--

Cape Cod Ornaments, Inc.
94 State Road
West Yarmouth, Massachusetts 02757

Dear Sirs:

I have seen your ad in the Boston Globe of Sunday, February 12, and would like to order the following weather vane:

Model EPC-18" eagle with arrow, copper, $34.95.

I would like the weather vane sent to the above address by parcel post and charged, with any applicable sales tax and handling costs, to my VISA account (number 003 0971 A109).

Yours truly,

Figure 3-2

ORDER

Reservations

Reservations for restaurants and theaters, nowadays, are often made by telephone while hotel reservations are speeded up by telegram (see Chapter 11). Still, whether made over the phone, in a brief telegram, or in a letter, all reservations must contain COMPLETE, ACCURATE INFORMATION.

Consider the following letter:

Gentlemen:

Please reserve a room for Ms. Lettman, who will be in Evansville October 27–29.

Yours truly,

Most hotels have a variety of accommodations as well as rates, and the sample letter gives a reservationist no hint about either. An effective reservation request (Figure 3-3) will specify:

1) the guest's full name;
2) the guest's company affiliation;
3) the dates of the stay (including an expected time of arrival);
4) the desired accommodations;
5) the preferred rate (or a special rate);

6) any special requirements;
7) a request for confirmation.

CONDO CORPORATION
209 West Street
Kingston, Jamaica, W.I.

October 2, 19--

The Executive Inn
2 Main Street
Evansville, Illinois 60821

Dear Sirs:

Please reserve a single room with bath for Ms. Linda Lettman for October 27–29. Ms. Lettman, general manager of the Condo Corporation, will arrive at the hotel at approximately 6 P.M. on October 27.

While in Evansville, Ms. Lettman will meet with six members of the local Chamber of Commerce. She would, therefore, like to reserve the use of a small conference room for the morning of October 28, from about 9 A.M. until noon.

Please let us know the rates for both Ms. Lettman's accommodations and the conference room, and confirm this reservation.

Truly yours,

Figure 3-3

RESERVATION REQUEST

★ PRACTICE CORRESPONDENCE

For each of the following activities, prepare a request letter using appropriate arrangement and punctuation styles.

A. You are the program chairperson of the Harrisburg Civic Association. Write a letter to Margaret Belmont, mayor of Harrisburg, asking if she would be willing to attend a future meeting of the association and address the members on a topic of general interest. Meetings are held the second Wednesday of every month at 7:30 P.M. in the basement meeting room of the community center. Previous speakers have included Raymond Delacorte, president of Grand Northern Motels, Inc., who spoke on the topic "Increasing Tourism in Harrisburg," and Gregory Lardas, CPA, who spoke on the topic "Local Property Tax: Boost or Burden?" You may explain that meetings are attended by approximately 75 community-minded people and that the lecture segment of the meeting usually lasts about one hour.

B. As assistant buyer for Fenway's Toy Store, 1704 North Broadway, Richmond, Virginia 23261, write a letter to the Marco Toy Company, Inc., 223 Sunrise Highway, Glen Cove, New York 11566, to order two dozen Baby Jenny dolls (at $10 each), one dozen Baby Jenny layette sets (at $15 each), and three dozen 18-inch Tootsie-Wootsie teddy bears (at $7 each). You would like to have these items in stock in time for the pre-Christmas selling season. You want to make this purchase on account and have it shipped air express. If Marco has available any special Christmas displays for their merchandise, you would like to receive these, too.

C. You will be attending a state-wide meeting of branch managers of the First Commercial Bank of Rhode Island. Therefore, write a letter to the Hotel Diplomat, 71 Front Street, Providence, Rhode Island 90911, to reserve a two-room suite. Because you will make a presentation to the branch managers from your hometown, you would like to arrange for the use of an overhead projector and screen for the afternoon of January 10. You plan to arrive at the hotel at about 5 P.M. on January 9 and stay until January 11. Request a confirmation and ask that your company be billed for your stay.

D. Answer the following advertisement in the current issue of *Office Workers' Weekly:*

COPY KWIK COPYHOLDER

America's widest used copyholders! Sturdy metal . . . calibrated . . . with See-Thru magnetic line guide. Makes all typing jobs faster and easier. In red, black, or white. Lifetime guarantee. $8.95 plus $1.25 postage and handling (N.J. residents please add appropriate sales tax). KKC, Inc., 2019 Logan Street, Paramus, NJ 70662.

E. You are the supervisor of the secretarial pool of the Am-Lux Company, Inc., 51 West 42 Street, New York, New York 10031. You recently read an article by Loretta Lawrence entitled "Ten Pitman Pitfalls to Watch Out For" in *Sten* magazine. You believe the twenty-five secretaries in your department would benefit from reading the article. Write a letter to Ms. Lawrence, in care of *Sten,* 705 Tenth Avenue, New York, New York 10048, requesting her permission to make twenty-five copies of her article for circulation only within your company.

4.
REPLIES

A large part of handling a company's correspondence involves ANSWER-
ING the mail. The ability to phrase an appropriate response is, therefore,
a valuable and marketable skill.

Letters of response fall into a number of categories, including:

1) acknowledgments
2) follow-ups
3) confirmations
4) remittances
5) order acknowledgments
6) stopgap letters
7) inquiry replies
8) referrals
9) refusals

Many companies use form letters for certain types of replies, such as order
acknowledgments. Nevertheless, a reply is often a fertile sales opportunity,
and a personal, carefully worded letter can reap both profits and goodwill.

Like a request, a reply should be *specific* and *complete.* However, a
reply need not be brief. Indeed, because a reply must be both *helpful* and
sales oriented, brevity is often impossible to achieve.

On the other hand, it is essential that a reply be *prompt.* In striving for
a *"you* approach," this promptness may even be pointed out to the reader:

Dear Mr. Mechanic:

I received your letter this morning and wanted to be sure
you would have our current price list before the end of the
week. . . .

Without patting yourself on the back, such an opening lets your reader know
you are *interested* and want to be *helpful.* In fact, whenever possible, a
response should go a little further than the original request. An extra bit of
information or unasked-for help can turn an inquirer into a steady customer.

Acknowledgments

An acknowledgment (Figure 4-1) should be written when you receive merchandise, material, money, or information. Such a letter is a courtesy, letting your reader know that his missal has reached its destination. When the matter received was not an order, an acknowledgment can also serve as a thank-you note.

MARKHAM'S CARDS AND GIFTS
400 Paseo de Peralta
Santa Fe, New Mexico 87501

October 23, 19--

Mr. Herbert Benjamin
Sales Representative
Newmart Cards, Inc.
399 North Canon Drive
Beverly Hills, California 90210

Dear Mr. Benjamin:

Thank you for arranging for us to receive our Christmas card displays a bit early this year. We installed them as soon as they arrived on Monday, and we've already sold out two lines!

The two months between now and Christmas seem destined to be busy ones, and I suspect you'll be hearing from us again soon.

Best wishes,

Hedy Rosen
Assistant Buyer

Figure 4-1

ACKNOWLEDGMENT

Follow-Ups

After a decision or agreement has been made, either at a meeting or in conversation, it is wise to send a follow-up letter (Figure 4-2) to establish a written record of the transaction.

THE COMMITTEE TO KEEP MINNESOTA GREEN
24 North Main Street
Blackduck, Minnesota 56630

June 3, 19--

Ms. Christine Solars
Solars, Solars, and Wright
62 Onigum Road
Walker, Minnesota 56484

Dear Ms. Solars:

We are pleased that you will be participating in the Ecology Colloquium sponsored by the Committee to Keep Minnesota Green. As we discussed in our telephone conversation this morning, the Colloquium will take place on June 29 in the convention room at the Blackduck Inn.

The Colloquium will begin with the keynote address at 10:30 A.M. At 11:00, you will join our other guests of honor in a debate on the topic, "The Cost of Conservation: Public or Private Responsibilities?" Following the debate, luncheon will be served in the main dining room, where you will, of course, be a guest of the Committee.

Along with the other members of the Committee, I am looking forward to our meeting on the 29th.

Sincerely yours,

Figure 4-2
FOLLOW-UP

Confirmations

While confirmations are routine for such businesses as hotels and travel agencies, other businesses may also require them. Doctors, for example, and repair services can avoid wasted time by contacting patients and customers a day or so in advance of scheduled appointments.

Professionals often confirm appointments by telephone, and many companies use form letters. Such methods are adequate for transmitting *clear, correct,* and *complete* information and are indispensable when the type of business requires large numbers of confirmations. Still, an individually written letter, such as Figure 4-3, adds a personal touch, that *extra effort,* that can turn a customer into a *regular* customer.

THE BARCLAY
5500 South 96th Street
Omaha, Nebraska 68127

August 10, 19--

Mr. Albert Durrell
2233 Connecticut Avenue, N.W.
Washington, D.C. 20008

Dear Mr. Durrell:

This letter will confirm your reservation for a single room with bath for August 24–27. Your room will be available after 2 P.M. on the 24th.

Since you will be arriving in Omaha by plane, you may want to take advantage of The Barclay's Shuttle. Our limousine departs from the domestic terminal every hour on the half hour, and the service is free for guests of the hotel.

Cordially yours,

Figure 4-3

CONFIRMATION

Remittances

Companies often request that their bill, or a portion of their bill, accompany a remittance. When this is not the case, a cover letter is necessary to explain what your enclosed check is for. This letter should contain any information regarding your order that will be needed for the proper crediting of your account: include your account number, the invoice number, and the amount of the check. DO NOT include superfluous information that could confuse an accounts receivable clerk. Remarks not directly related to the remittance should be reserved for a separate letter.

Dear Sirs:

The enclosed check for $312.68 is in payment of invoice no. 10463. Please credit my account (no. 663-711-M).

Yours truly,

Order Acknowledgments

Many companies today have abandoned the practice of acknowledging orders, particularly when the order will be filled promptly. Some companies respond to orders by immediately sending an invoice, and some employ the halfway measure of using printed acknowledgment forms. But however handled, confirming an order helps to establish goodwill by reassuring the customer that the order has been received.

First orders SHOULD be acknowledged in order to welcome the new customer and encourage further business (Figure 4-4). Similarly, an unusually large order by a regular customer deserves a note of appreciation.

Any order acknowledgment, whatever the circumstances, should contain specific information. It should let the customer know exactly what is being done about the order by

1) mentioning the date of the order;
2) including the order or invoice number;
3) explaining the date and method of shipment;
4) acknowledging the method of payment.

Of course, all order acknowledgments should also express appreciation for the order and assure the customer that it will be filled.

An acknowledgment is often an opportunity for a salespitch. First of all, if a salesperson was involved in the order, his or her name should appear somewhere in the letter. But beyond this, a letter may also include a description of the merchandise to reaffirm the wisdom of the customer's purchase. Other related products may also be mentioned to spark the customer's interest and future orders.

Because orders cannot always be filled promptly and smoothly, situations arise in which a wise businessperson will send more than a mere acknowledgment.

Customers, for example, cannot always be relied on to submit complete orders. When an essential piece of information has been omitted, the order must be delayed and a tactful letter sent. Although the customer in such a case is at fault, the letter must neither place any blame nor express impatience. Indeed, the customer's own impatience must be allayed with a positive, friendly tone. A bit of reselling—reminding the customer of the order's desirability—is often in order in a letter of this kind.

Dear Mr. Norton:

Thank you for your order of October 22 for 6 rolls of black nylon webbing. We are eager to deliver Order 129 to your store as soon as possible.

But first, please let us know whether you'd like the webbing in 1-, 1⅓-, or 2½-inch widths. If you note your preference on the bottom of this letter and mail it back to us today, we can have your order ready by the beginning of next week.

Olsen's Upholstery products are among the finest made, and we're sure you'd like to receive your purchase without further delay.

Sincerely yours,

PAYTON'S PLASTICS, INC.
1313 Spruce Street
Philadelphia, PA 17512

September 16, 19--

FRAMES-BY-YOU
126 Walnut Street
Philadelphia, PA 17503

ATTENTION: MS. CYBEL MEGAN

Dear Sirs:

We are pleased to have received your order of September 15 and would like to welcome you as a new customer of Payton's Plastics.

Your order (No. 62997) for one dozen 4' × 5' sheets of ⅛" Lucite is being processed and will be ready for shipment on September 21. It will be delivered to your workshop by our own van, and payment will be c.o.d. (our policy for all orders under $100).

We are sure you will appreciate the clear finish and tensile strength of our entire line of plastics. Ms. Julie Methel, your sales representative, will call on you soon with a catalog and samples.

Cordially,

PAYTON'S PLASTICS, INC.

Howard Roberts
Customer Relations

Figure 4-4

ORDER ACKNOWLEDGMENT

Sometimes a *delayed delivery* is caused by the seller, not the buyer—a delicate situation that requires a carefully written letter (Figure 4-5). When an order cannot be filled promptly, the customer is entitled to an explanation. Assurance should be given that the delay is unavoidable and that everything is being done to speed delivery.

Such a letter must be especially *"you*-oriented." It should express that you understand the customer's disappointment and regret the inconvenience. At the same time, the letter must avoid a negative tone and not only stress that the merchandise is worth waiting for, but assume that the customer is willing to wait.

AMERICAN ELECTRIC COMPANY, INC.
1066 Third Avenue
New York, New York 10081

Dear

Requests for our pamphlet, "10 Points to Consider When Buying Home Video Equipment," have been overwhelming. As a result, we are temporarily out of copies.

Nevertheless, the new printing is presently being prepared, and I have added your name to the mailing list to receive a copy as soon as it is available.

In the meantime, you may find an article by Professor Leonard Mack, of the Pennsylvania Institute of Technology, to be of some help. The article, entitled "The Latest Crop of Home Video Centers," appeared in the September issue of Consumer Digest.

Sincerely,

Figure 4-5

DELAYED DELIVERY

SILVER IMPORTS, LTD.
609 San Anselmo Avenue
San Anselmo, California 94960

March 4, 19--

Ms. Bonnie Corum
Bonnie's Baubles
4091 West Ninth Street
Winston-Salem, North Carolina 27102

Dear Ms. Corum:

Thank you for your recent order, number 622. We are always especially delighted to serve an old friend.

Your six pairs of Chinese Knot earrings (item 15b) and one dozen
Primrose pendants (item 8a) have been shipped by United Parcel and
should arrive at your boutique within the week.

Unfortunately, our stock of cloisonné bangle bracelets (item 9d) has
been depleted because of a delay in shipments from China. Our
craftsmen have been at great pains to keep up with the demand for
these intricate and finely wrought bracelets. We have put your one
dozen bracelets on back order and hope to have them on their way to
you before the end of the month.

Very truly yours,

Chun Lee Ng
Manager

Figure 4-6

PARTIAL DELIVERY

When a *partial shipment* can be made, the customer must be informed
that certain items have been *back ordered.* Again, the letter should assume
the customer's willingness to wait. But it should also make an attempt to
"resell" the merchandise by stressing its finer features without emphasizing
the missing items (see Figure 4-6).

When an order cannot be filled at all, a letter suggesting a *substitute
order* (Figure 4-7) is occasionally appropriate. The suggested merchandise
must, naturally, be comparable to the original order and should be offered
from a perspective, not of salvaging a sale, but of helping the customer. The
letter must include a sales pitch for the suggested item, but it should emphasize the customer's needs. Of course, the letter should also explain why the
original order cannot be filled.

BOOKS-BY-MAIL
P.O. Box 799
Dallas, Texas 75220

April 10, 19--

Mrs. Donna Phillips
RFD 2
Crosby, Texas 77532

Dear Mrs. Phillips:

Thank you so much for ordering Indra Madhur's outstanding book, An Introduction to Indian Cooking. As you know, in the fifteen years since its first publication, Mr. Madhur's book has become a classic and a standard for great cooks everywhere.

Sadly, An Introduction is no longer in print, and I am returning your check for $15.95. But to satisfy your interest in Indian cuisine, I would like to suggest an alternative, Purnamattie Jaffre's Indian Gourmet. Ms. Jaffre was a student of Mr. Madhur, and her recently published volume has been widely hailed by both food and cookbook critics.

If you would like a copy of Indian Gourmet, which costs only $13.95, please let me know, and I will immediately send it to you.

Cordially,

David Ewing
Order Department

Figure 4-7

SUBSTITUTE DELIVERY

Stopgap Letters

When a thorough response to an incoming letter must be delayed, receipt of the letter at least should be promptly acknowledged. Such letters of acknowledgment are called STOPGAP LETTERS. They let your correspondent know that his inquiry has not been ignored and will be attended to as soon as possible.

Like a delayed delivery letter, a stopgap letter informs your customer that time is needed to process his request. Necessary information or materials, for example, may not be immediately available. Or your company may have prescribed channels for reacting to certain inquiries. Credit applications and insurance claims, for instance, take time to be processed and so are often answered promptly with a stopgap acknowledgment.

A stopgap letter will also be called for when your employer is out of town. The correspondent should be assured that his letter will be relayed to your employer as soon as he returns. You should be careful NOT to commit your employer to any action, nor should you explain his absence.

Dear Reverend Hollingsworth:

Your request to meet with Rabbi Tucker to discuss his participating in an interfaith symposium on world peace arrived this morning. However, Rabbi Tucker is out of town and is not expected back before the 15th.

I will be sure to inform Rabbi Tucker of the planned symposium as soon as he returns.

Yours truly,

Inquiry Replies

All inquiries should be answered, even those that cannot for some reason be given a complete response. An inquiry indicates interest in your company and a potential customer. The inquiry reply should be designed not only to increase that interest, but to inspire the inquirer to action.

An inquiry reply should begin by thanking the reader, acknowledging the interest in your company. As in Figure 4-8, it should end by offering further assistance—but ONLY if you actually want additional inquiries from this person.

The substance of an inquiry reply is usually *information.* You should include not just the specific facts your correspondent requested, but any others that may be of help. (This is, of course, assuming that the original inquiry or request was reasonable.) If you cannot provide all the relevant data right away, you should promise it.

A & M SEWING SUPPLIES, INC.
40-04 Summit Avenue
Fairlawn, NJ 07662

June 2, 19--

Mr. Samuel Long
Maxine Sportswear Manufacturing Co., Inc.
842 Seventh Avenue
New York, New York 10018

Dear Mr. Long:

Thank you for your interest in A & M equipment. We are happy to
supply you with the information you requested.

The following prices are quoted per dozen. Individual units are
slightly higher:

Item	1 Dozen @:
A-1 Garment Turner	$125.00
A-1 Automatic Winder	59.00
Ace Thread Trimmer	85.00
No-Slip Feed Puller	98.00

In case you have any further questions, Mr. Long, please do not
hesitate to call. I can be reached between 8:30 A.M. and 6:00 P.M. at
(201) 881-9412.

Sincerely yours,

Figure 4-8

INQUIRY REPLY I

If the information requested cannot be provided at all (as in Figure 4-9),
if it is confidential, you should explain this in your letter. You must be careful,
however, to word your explanation tactfully and resist the impulse to accuse
your reader of trying to gather information to which she is not entitled.
Assume the inquiry was innocent and try to maintain goodwill.

MAXINE SPORTSWEAR MANUFACTURING CO., INC.
842 Seventh Avenue
New York, New York 10018

June 10, 19--

Mrs. Sharon Klein
693 Pelham Parkway
Bronx, New York 10422

Dear Mrs. Klein:

We certainly appreciate your interest in Maxine Sportswear. Nevertheless, I am afraid I cannot supply you with the information you request.

Because we do not sell our garments directly to the consumer, we try to keep our wholesale prices between ourselves and our dealers. It is our way of meriting both the loyalty and good faith of those with whom we do business. Clearly, divulging our wholesale prices to a consumer would be a violation of a trust.

However, I have enclosed for your reference a list of our dealers in the Bronx and Manhattan. A number of these dealers sell Maxine Sportswear at discount.

Very truly yours,

Figure 4-9

INQUIRY REPLY II

Sometimes a request for information about a company's products or services may be answered with a brochure or catalog. Such materials, though, must always be accompanied by a personalized cover letter. You should not only explain why you've sent the brochure and arouse your reader's interest in it; you should also call attention to particulars of the brochure and attempt to encourage a sale.

A good practice for a manufacturer, moreover, who doesn't sell directly to the public, is to pass along copies of the inquiry and reply to a dealer, who may pursue the sale further.

Dear Mr. Godonov:

Thank you for your request for information about the Teaneck Tennis Center. One of New Jersey's newest facilities, we are a full-service tennis club just 15 minutes from Manhattan.

The enclosed brochure describes our special features, including championship-size courts and professional instruction. You may find the section on our Businessmen's Special of particular interest.

If you drop by Teaneck Tennis anytime between 7 A.M. and 10 P.M., we would be delighted to give you a personal tour of the Center--at no obligation of course.

Cordially yours,

Referrals

Business people often receive inquiries that can best be answered by another person. In that case, the correspondent must be informed that the inquiry is being passed on.

A letter of referral should *acknowledge receipt* of the inquiry and *explain* why and to whom it is being referred. Alternately, you may find it more efficient to advise the correspondent of the proper source of information and tell exactly where to write.

Again, a manufacturer should be especially careful to sustain the reader's interest even while referring her to a dealer. The address of a local dealer or a list of dealers in the area should be included in this kind of referral. Too, the reader should *never* be chastised for bypassing the middleman; instead, she should be politely referred to the appropriate source.

Dear Mrs. Simpson:

Your request for information regarding marriage counselors in your community can best be answered by the Board of Community Services.

I am therefore referring your letter to Mr. Orlando Ortiz at the Whitestone Community Board. He will, I am sure, be in touch with you soon.

Yours truly,

Refusals

There are many times when a businessperson must say no. When granting a favor, awarding a contract, hiring an applicant, or for that matter making any decision, saying yes to one person often means saying no to another. The key, however, is to say no gracefully. Here, as in most correspondence, maintaining goodwill is extremely important.

When saying no, you should first of all never actually say *no.* Your letter should be as positive as you can make it. The actual refusal should be stated once and briefly. The rest of the letter should be reader oriented and very friendly.

No matter what the request, your reader deserves an explanation of your refusal. Your reason should be based on facts, not emotions, although an appeal to your reader's sense of fair play or business savvy is often appropriate (see Figure 4-10). NEVER make the reader himself the reason for your refusal.

Rarely will you want in a refusal to sever all business connections. Therefore, you should be careful to keep your letter "open-ended." Express appreciation for the request though it is being denied, and if possible suggest an alternative course of action. A "not-at-this-time" refusal keeps open the possibility of future business.

AGNES CAFIERO, M.D.
California Institute of Psychiatry
629 Seventh Avenue
San Francisco, California 94120

September 1, 19--

The Honorable Nelson McKenzie
The State Capitol Building
Sacramento, California 91400

Dear Mr. McKenzie:

Thank you for your recent request for my endorsement of your campaign for United States Senator. I am honored that you believe my name could be of value to you.

My professional policy, however, is to refrain from public endorsements. In my practice, I treat patients of all political parties, and I strongly believe that it is in their best interest that I maintain a nonpartisan position.

Privately, of course, I allow myself more leeway. I have always been impressed by your stand on the issues, particularly your support of the Equal Rights Amendment. I wish you all the best in your campaign and am enclosing a personal contribution of $100.

Sincerely yours,

Agnes Cafiero, M.D.

Figure 4-10
REFUSAL

★ PRACTICE CORRESPONDENCE

Prepare a letter of response for each of the following situations on another sheet of paper.

A. You are employed in the shipping department of Kinbote Products, Inc., 200 Southeast Fourth Street, Miami, Florida 33131. Write a letter acknowledging the following order from Ellen Minsky, buyer for Gold's Specialty Shops, 3636 West Grace Street, Tampa, Florida 33607.

Dear Sirs:

Please send me two dozen exercise suits (Style L-29) in the following assortment of sizes and colors:

Vanilla--3 petite, 3 small, 4 medium, 2 large
Chocolate--2 petite, 4 small, 4 medium, 2 large

Charge my account (882GSS) for the wholesale price of $22 per suit.

I would like the order shipped air express and would appreciate your letting me know how soon I may expect delivery.

Yours truly,

B. Cornell Peal, vice-president of the General Communications Corporation, 600 North Milwaukee Street, Milwaukee, Wisconsin 53202, is out of town attending a four-day meeting of the regional directors of the company. As his administrative assistant, send a stopgap letter in response to the following request from Professor Anne Boleyn, Department of Media and Communications, University of Wisconsin, Menomonie, Wisconsin 54751.

Dear Mr. Peal:

Last month, I telephoned your office to invite you to give a guest lecture to my graduate seminar in teletronics. You said you would be pleased to give such a lecture but asked that I contact you again, in writing, later in the semester.

If you are still interested in visiting the class, I would very much like to set a date for the lecture. The class meets on Tuesdays from 4:30 to 6:00 P.M. and runs for six more weeks.

I would appreciate your letting me know as soon as possible which Tuesday would be most convenient for you.

Sincerely yours,

C. You have just made a luncheon engagement for your employer Nancy Carson, an architect with Fulson Contractors, Inc., 4444 Western Avenue, Boulder, Colorado 80301. The appointment is with a prospective client, Justin Michaels, 622 Garth Street, Boulder, Colorado 80321. Write a letter to Mr. Michaels to confirm the lunch date, which will take place at Trattoria di Marco, at the corner of Tenth Street and Western Avenue, on April 7 at 1 P.M.

D. You are employed by the Lawsen Linen Company, P.O. Box 762, Bloomfield, New Jersey 07003. Write a letter to Mrs. Marianne Rollins, 444 Ross Avenue, Caldwell, New Jersey 07006, to explain a delay in shipping her order for one set of Floral Mist queen-size sheets and pillowcases. Because of a factory strike, all orders have been held up, but assure her that negotiations are progressing and a settlement is expected soon. Convince her to wait and not cancel her order.

E. Arthur Edwards, owner of Edwards Drug Store, 1540 Peachtree Street, N.E., Atlanta, Georgia 30309, has been a customer of the Southern Cosmetics Company, 2109 Lenox Road, N.E., Atlanta, Georgia 30326, for seven years. Because Mr. Edwards has placed an unusually large order, he has requested a special discount. As a representative of Southern Cosmetics, write a letter to Mr. Edwards refusing the discount.

5.
CREDIT AND
COLLECTION LETTERS

Credit Letters

Credit involves the purchasing and receiving of goods without immediate payment. Being able to "buy now and pay later" enables a purchaser to acquire desired goods even when cash is not currently available. Allowing individuals and businesses to buy on credit can increase a company's volume of sales. Therefore, buying and selling on credit have become a common and essential business practice.

Of course, before granting credit, a company must be reasonably sure of the customer's financial stability, her ability and willingness to pay. These are verified by the exchange of credit information. Five types of letters are involved in credit correspondence:

1) applications for credit
2) inquiries about credit worthiness
3) responses about credit worthiness
4) letters granting credit
5) letters refusing credit

APPLICATIONS

Consumer applications for charge accounts, with businesses such as department stores or gasoline companies, are usually made by filling out an application blank. This form typically allows space for home and business addresses, names of banks and account numbers, a list of other charge accounts, and, perhaps, a list of references.

Business account applications are more often made by letter (Figure 5-1). A new business, for example, may wish to place a first order with a supplier or manufacturer and establish a credit line or open account. A letter of this kind should include credit references (such as banks and other businesses that have extended credit).

CREDIT INQUIRIES

Department stores usually turn credit applications over to a *credit bureau*. Such bureaus keep files on people and businesses whose credit references and histories they have investigated. When they determine an applicant's *credit standing* (that is, reputation for financial stability), they give the applicant a *credit rating* (the bureau's evaluation of the credit standing). On the

49

KRETCHMER'S APPLIANCE STORE
1135 State Street
Chicago, Illinois 60688

February 3, 19--

Standard Electric Corporation
2120 Oak Terrace
Lake Bluff, Illinois 60044

Dear Sirs:

Enclosed is our purchase order 121 for 6 four-slice toasters, model 18E.

We would like to place this order on open account according to your regular terms. Our store has been open for two months, and you may check our credit rating with Ms. Peggy Sawyer, branch manager of the First Bank of Chicago, 1160 State Street, Chicago, Illinois 60688.

You may also check our credit standing with the following companies:

The Kenso Clock Company, 150 Ottawa, N.W., Grand Rapids, Michigan 49503

National Kitchen Products, Inc., 55 East Main Street, Round Lake Park, Illinois 60733

Eastern Electric Corporation, 750 East 58 Street, Chicago, Illinois 60637

Please let us know your decision regarding our credit as well as an approximate delivery date for our first order.

Sincerely yours,

Bruce Kretchmer

Figure 5-1

CREDIT APPLICATION

basis of this rating, the store decides whether or not to grant the applicant credit.

When checking a business's credit standing, a company may contact the references directly. The letter of credit inquiry (see Figure 5-2) should contain all known information about the applicant, and it should assure the reference that all information will remain confidential. The inclusion of a reply envelope is a wise courtesy.

STANDARD ELECTRIC CORPORATION
2120 Oak Terrace
Lake Bluff, Illinois 60044

February 7, 19--

Ms. Peggy Sawyer
Branch Manager
The First Bank of Chicago
1160 State Street
Chicago, Illinois 60688

Dear Ms. Sawyer:

Kretchmer's Appliance Store, 1135 State Street, Chicago, has placed an order with us for $120 worth of merchandise and listed you as a credit reference.

We would appreciate your sending us information regarding Kretchmer's credit rating. We would especially like to know how long the owner, Bruce Kretchmer, has had an account with you and whether or not any of his debts are past due. We will, of course, keep any information we receive in the strictest confidence.

A reply envelope is enclosed for your convenience.

Sincerely yours,

STANDARD ELECTRIC CORPORATION

Milton Smedley
Credit Department

Figure 5-2

CREDIT INQUIRY

CREDIT RESPONSES

Companies that receive large numbers of credit inquiries often use their own form for responding. In this way, they can control the information given out and, especially, limit the information to hard facts: amounts owed and presently due, maximum credit allowed, dates of account's opening and last sale, degree of promptness in payment, etc.

Because an individual's or business's reputation is at stake, opinions should be expressed discreetly, if at all. Particularly when a credit reference is unfavorable, it is advisable to state only objective facts in order to avoid a possible libel suit. Most companies, moreover, reiterate somewhere in the letter (see Figure 5-3) that they expect the information provided to remain confidential.

THE FIRST BANK OF CHICAGO
1160 State Street
Chicago, Illinois 60688

February 14, 19--

Mr. Milton Smedley
Credit Department
Standard Electric Corporation
2120 Oak Terrace
Lake Bluff, Illinois 60044

Dear Mr. Smedley:

We are happy to send you, in confidence, the credit information you requested concerning Mr. Bruce Kretchmer, owner of Kretchmer's Appliance Store.

Mr. Kretchmer, who was appliance department supervisor at Lillian's Department Store until last fall, has had personal checking and savings accounts with us for the past ten years. His accounts were always in order, with adequate balances to cover all checks drawn.

His appliance store, at 1135 State Street, was opened last December. For this undertaking, he borrowed $8,000 from this bank and has begun making regular payments against the loan. We are unaware of any further outstanding debts he may have.

On the basis of our experience with him, we believe Mr. Kretchmer to be credit worthy.

Yours truly,

THE FIRST BANK OF CHICAGO

Peggy Sawyer
Branch Manager

Figure 5-3
CREDIT REFERENCE

CREDIT-GRANTING LETTERS

When all credit references are favorable, a letter is sent granting credit to the customer (Figure 5-4). Whether for a consumer charge account or a dealer open account, the acceptance letter should:

1) approve the credit;
2) welcome the customer and express appreciation;
3) explain the credit terms and privileges;
4) establish goodwill and encourage further sales.

STANDARD ELECTRIC CORPORATION
2120 Oak Terrace
Lake Bluff, Illinois 60044

February 18, 19--

Mr. Bruce Kretchmer
Kretchmer's Appliance Store
1135 State Street
Chicago, Illinois 60688

Dear Mr. Kretchmer:

It is my pleasure to welcome you as an SEC credit customer, for your request for credit has been approved.

Your first order, for 6 Model 18E toasters, will be ready for shipment on Monday, February 22.

On the first of each month, we will prepare a statement of the previous month's purchases. Your payment is due in full on the tenth. With each statement, you will also receive a supply of order forms and return envelopes.

Arlene Ryan, your personal SEC sales representative, will visit you some time next week. In addition to bringing you catalogs and samples, she will explain our special dealer options, such as advertising campaigns and rebate programs.

We are delighted that SEC can be a part of your store's beginnings and look forward to serving you for many years to come.

Sincerely yours,

Milton Smedley
Credit Department

Figure 5-4

CREDIT-GRANTING LETTER

CREDIT-REFUSING LETTERS

Sometimes, of course, credit must be denied (Figure 5-5). A letter refusing credit must give the customer a reason, which, however, may be expressed vaguely for purposes of tact and protection of references.

The credit-refusal letter must also try to encourage business on a cash basis; the tone, therefore, must be positive and in some way *"you-*oriented."* In addition, it is a good idea to suggest that the customer reapply for credit in the future, thereby letting him know that you nevertheless desire and appreciate his business.

HANS & MEYER'S
1010 Broadway
New York, NY 10033

August 10, 19--

Mr. Donald Cortland
20-67 Kissena Blvd.
Queens, NY 11203

Dear Mr. Cortland:

Thank you for your recent application for a Hans & Meyer charge account. However, we believe it would not be in your best interest to grant you credit at this time.

An impartial credit investigation indicates that your present financial obligations are substantial. We fear that adding to those obligations could jeopardize your sound credit standing in the community.

Of course, Mr. Cortland, you are always welcome to shop at Hans & Meyer's, where we will try our best to serve you in anyway possible. And if, in the future, your obligations should be reduced, feel free to apply again for a charge account. We shall be delighted to reconsider.

Cordially yours,

Figure 5-5

CREDIT-REFUSING LETTER

Collection Letters

No matter how carefully a company screens its credit customers, there will be times when a bill goes unpaid and steps to collect must be taken. The problem when writing a collection letter is how to exact payment and simultaneously keep a customer. The writer of a collection letter wants to get the money owed *and* maintain goodwill.

Collection letters, therefore, should be *persuasive* rather than forceful, *firm* rather than demanding. A fair and tactful letter gets better results than a sarcastic or abusive one. In fact, even collection letters should be *"you-oriented"*: courteous, considerate, and concerned about the customer's best interest.

Collection letters are usually sent in a series. The first tend to be mildest and most understanding, with the letters getting gradually more insistent. The final letter in a series, when all else has failed, threatens to turn the matter over to a lawyer or collection agency. Of course, the tone of any letter in the series will vary, from positive and mild to negative and strong, depending upon the past payment record of the particular customer. The intervals between the letters may also vary, from ten days to a month at the start, from one to two weeks later on.

Every letter in a collection series should contain certain information:

1) the amount owed;
2) how long the bill is overdue;
3) a specific action the customer may take.

Some companies also like to include a SALES APPEAL, even late in the series, as an extra incentive for payment.

The majority of bills are paid within ten days of receipt, with nearly all the rest being paid within the month. Therefore, when a bill is a month overdue, action is called for. Still, the collection process must begin gently.

STEP 1

The *monthly statement* reminds the customer of outstanding bills. If it is ignored, it should be followed (about a week or ten days later) by a second statement. The second statement should contain a notice (in the form of a rubber stamp or sticker) stating "Past Due" or "Please Remit." An alternative is to include a card or slip with the statement, alerting the customer to the overdue bill. This notice should be phrased in formal, possibly even stilted language; it is an *objective* reminder that does not embarrass the customer with too early a personal appeal.

> Our records indicate that the balance of $_____ on your account is now past due. Payment is requested.

STEP 2

If the objective statement and reminder fail to get results, the collection process must gradually become more emotional and personal. (Form letters may be used, but they should *look* personal, adapted to the specific situation, perhaps even originally typed.) The second collection message, however, should still be friendly. It should seek to excuse the unpaid bill as an oversight; the tone should convey the assumption that the customer intends to pay. At this stage, too, a stress on future sales, rather than on payment, may induce action.

Collection Letter I

Dear _____ :

Snow may still be on the ground, but the first signs of spring are already budding. And we know you will be planning your Spring Sales soon. You may already have your order in mind.

When you send us a check for $_____, now _____ _____ past due, you will guarantee that your next order will be promptly filled.

Oversights, of course, do happen, but we know you won't want to miss the opportunity, not only of stocking up for the coming season, but of taking advantage of our seasonal ad campaign as well.

Sincerely yours,

STEP 3

The next letter in the series should still be friendly, but it should also now be firm. While expressing confidence in the customer's intention to pay, it should inquire about the *reason* for the delay. The third collection message should also make an appeal to the customer's sense of:

1) fairness;
2) cooperation;
3) obligation;

or desire to:

1) save her credit reputation;
2) maintain her credit line.

This letter should stress the customer's self-interest by pointing out the importance of prompt payment and the dangers of losing credit standing. The letter should convey the urgency and seriousness of the situation.

Collection Letter II

Dear _____ :

We are truly at a loss. We cannot understand why you still have not cleared your balance of $_____, which is now _____ overdue.

Although you have been a reliable customer for _____ years, we are afraid you are placing your credit standing in jeopardy. Only you, by sending us a check today, can insure your reputation and secure the continued convenience of buying on credit.

We would hate to lose a valued friend, Mr./Ms. _____. Please allow us to keep serving you.

Sincerely,

STEP 4

Ultimately, payment must be demanded. The threat of legal action or the intervention of a collection agency is sometimes all that will induce a customer to pay. In some companies, moreover, an executive other than the credit manager signs this last letter as a means of impressing the customer with the finality of the situation. Still, the fourth collection letter should allow the customer one last chance to pay before steps are taken.

Final Collection Letter

Dear _____ :

Our Collection Department has informed me of their intention to file suit as you have failed to answer any of our requests for payment of $_____ , which is now _____ overdue.

Before taking this action, however, I would like to make a personal appeal to your sound business judgment. I feel certain that, if you telephone me, we can devise some means to settle this matter out of court.

Therefore, I ask that you get in touch with me by the _____ of the month so that I may avoid taking steps which neither of us would like.

Truly yours,

Note: If a customer responds to a collection letter, STOP THE COLLECTION SERIES, even if the response is not full payment.

A customer may, for example, offer an excuse or promise payment; he may make a partial payment or request special arrangements. At this point, the series would be inappropriate.

For instance, if your customer has owed $600 on account for two months and sends you a check for $150, you may send a letter such as the following:

Dear Mr. Marsh:

Thank you for your check for $150. The balance remaining on your account is now $450.

Since you have requested an extension, we offer you the following payment plan: $150 by the 15th of the month for the next three months.

If you have another plan in mind, please telephone my office so that we may discuss it. Otherwise, we will expect your next check for $150 on September 15.

Sincerely yours,

★ PRACTICE CORRESPONDENCE

For each of the following, prepare a credit or collection letter, as specified in the directions.

A. Mr. Marvin Gold of 1602 Arlington Avenue, Bronx, New York 10477, has had a charge account at Manson's Department Store, 4404 Madison Avenue, New York, New York 10008, for six years. His credit limit is $400. He has always paid his bills on time although he currently has an outstanding balance of $182.54, forty-five days overdue. The National Credit Bureau has contacted Manson's for credit information about Mr. Gold. Write the letter Manson's should send to the National Credit Bureau.

B. The credit references of Ms. Migdalia Ruiz (818 Ocean Parkway, Brooklyn, New York 11202) are all favorable, and so her new charge account with Manson's Department Store has been approved. Write the letter Manson's should send to Ms. Ruiz.

C. Ms. Hiroko Osawa's credit references indicate that, although she has no outstanding debts or record of poor payment, her employment history is unstable. Manson's Department Store, therefore, concludes that she would be a poor credit risk. Write the letter that Manson's should send to Ms. Osawa (6061 Valentine Lane, Yonkers, New York 80301), denying her application for a charge account.

D. Weimar's Furniture Emporium (617 Sherman Road, North Hollywood, California 91605) has owed the Eastgate Furniture Manufacturing Company, Inc., $750 for forty-five days. Eastgate has sent two statements and one letter, which Weimar's has ignored. Write the next letter that Eastgate (305 Bush Street, San Francisco, California 94108) should send to Weimar's.

E. For eight years, Mr. Josef Larsen, of 1 Penny Lane, Summit, Pennsylvania 17214, has been a charge customer of Browne's Department Store (900 Chestnut Street, Philadelphia, Pennsylvania 19107). A "slow pay," he has nevertheless always remitted within sixty days of purchase. However, Mr. Larsen's balance of $269.48 is now ninety days past due. He has not responded to the two statements and two letters Browne's has already sent him. Write the next letter that Browne's should send to Mr. Larsen.

6.
CLAIMS AND ADJUSTMENTS

Business transactions will from time to time go awry, and the exchange of money, merchandise, or service will not occur as expected. In such situations, the customer must promptly notify the company of the problem; the letter written is called a *claim*. The company, responding to the claim, will write a letter of *adjustment*.

Claims

Countless aspects of business dealings can break down, but the most common causes for claims are:

1) an incorrect bill, invoice, or statement (Figure 6-1);
2) a bill for merchandise ordered but never received;
3) delivery of unordered merchandise;
4) delivery of incorrect merchandise;
5) delivery of damaged or defective merchandise (Figure 6-2);
6) an unusually delayed delivery.

Two other more specialized types of claims are:

1) a request for an adjustment under a guarantee or warranty;
2) a request for restitution under an insurance policy.

A claim is written to *inform* the company of the problem and *suggest* a fair compensation. No matter how infuriating the nature of the problem nor how great the inconvenience, the purpose of a claim is NOT to express anger, but to get results.

Therefore, it is important to avoid a hostile or demanding tone. A claim must be calm and polite though, of course, also firm.

A claim should begin with the facts, first explaining the problem (such as the condition of the merchandise or the specific error made). Then all the necessary details should be recounted in a logical order. These details may include the order and delivery dates, the order or invoice number, the account number, the method of shipment, etc. A copy of proof of purchase, such as a sales slip or an invoice, should be included whenever possible. (Always, of course, retain the original.)

Remember: You are more likely to receive a favorable response from an adjuster who understands your problem thoroughly.

The second part of a claim should emphasize the loss or inconvenience that has been suffered. Again, the account should be factual and unemotional, and naturally you should NOT exaggerate.

Finally, you should state a *reasonable* adjustment. This should be worded positively and convey your confidence that the company will be fair.

As you read the following sample claims, notice especially how they state all the *facts calmly. The writer never loses his or her temper, never makes a threat, and never attempts to place blame.* At all times, the letter is directed toward the solution.

---

811 Regent Street
Phoenix, Arizona 99087
December 3, 19--

Gleason's Department Store
2297 Front Street
Phoenix, Arizona 99065

Dear Sirs:

I have just received the November statement on my charge account (No. 059-3676). The statement lists a purchase for $83.95, including tax, which I am sure I did not make.

This purchase was supposedly made in Department 08 on November 12. But because I was out of town the week of the tenth and no one else is authorized to use my account, I am sure the charge is in error.

I have checked all the other items on the statement against my sales receipts, and they all seem to be correct. I am therefore deducting the $83.95 from the balance on the statement and sending you a check for $155.75.

I would appreciate your looking into this matter so that my account may be cleared.

Sincerely yours,

Figure 6-1

CLAIM I

JACK'S HARDWARE STORE
72 Elm Street
Kennebunk, Maine 06606

April 12, 19--

Eterna-Tools, Inc.
Route 9
Saddlebrook, New Jersey 07666

Dear Sirs:

On March 1, we ordered and subsequently received one case of handsaws, model 88b. We paid for the order with our check no. 7293, a photocopy of which is enclosed.

When we decided to order these saws instead of model 78b, it was at the urging of your sales representative, Harold Saunders. He assured us that the new saws were more durable and efficient than the older model.

However, we have now had the saws on our selling floor for three weeks, and already six have been returned with broken teeth by extremely dissatisfied customers.

We are therefore returning the entire order of 88b saws and would like to be refunded for their full purchase price plus shipping expenses.

Yours truly,

Figure 6-2
CLAIM II

Adjustments

Claims should be answered *promptly* with a letter that will restore the customer's goodwill and confidence in the company. Like a claim, a letter of *adjustment* should emphasize the solution rather than the error and convince the customer that you understand and want to be fair.

An adjustment letter should begin with a positive statement, expressing sympathy and understanding. Near the start, it should let the reader know what is being done, and this news, good or bad, should be followed by an explanation. The letter should end with another positive statement, reaffirming the company's good intentions and the value of its products, but NEVER referring to the original problem.

Whether or not your company is at fault, even the most belligerent claim should be answered politely. An adjustment letter should NOT be negative or suspicious; it must NEVER accuse the customer or grant any adjustment grudgingly. Remember, your company's image and goodwill are at stake when you respond even to unjustified claims.

When the facts of a claim have been confirmed, one of three fair solutions are possible:

1) The requested adjustment is granted.
2) A compromise adjustment is proposed.
3) Any adjustment is denied.

Responsibility for the problem, reliability of the customer, and the nature of the business relationship are all considered in determining a fair adjustment. But the ultimate settlement must always be within the bounds of *company policy*.

GRANTING AN ADJUSTMENT

This letter should be cheerful, freely admitting errors and willingly offering the adjustment. It should express appreciation for the information provided in the claim. The letter *may* include an explanation of what went wrong; it *should* include an indication that similar errors will be unlikely in the future. Finally, it should *resell* the company, perhaps by suggesting future business (see Figure 6-3).

GLEASON'S DEPARTMENT STORE
2297 Front Street
Phoenix, Arizona 99065

December 8, 19--

Ms. Rosetta Falco
811 Regent Street
Phoenix, Arizona 99087

Dear Ms. Falco:

As you mentioned in your letter of December 3, you were indeed billed for a purchase you had not made.

According to our records, you should not have been charged the $83.95, and the sum has been stricken from your account.

Thank you for bringing this matter to our attention. We hope you have not been inconvenienced and will visit Gleason's soon so that we may again have the pleasure to serve you.

Sincerely yours,

Figure 6-3

LETTER OF ADJUSTMENT I

OFFERING A COMPROMISE ADJUSTMENT

This letter will be written when neither the company nor the customer is entirely at fault. It must express an attitude of pleasant cooperation. It should be based on facts and offer a reason for refusing the requested adjustment. As in Figure 6-4, it should immediately make a counteroffer that meets the customer halfway. Of course, it should leave the decision to accept the adjustment to the customer and suggest a course of action.

ETERNA-TOOLS, INC.
Route 9
Saddlebrook, N.J. 07666

April 19. 19--

Mr. Jack Patterson
Jack's Hardware Store
72 Elm Street
Kennebunk, Maine 06606

Dear Mr. Patterson:

We are sorry that the model 88b handsaws you purchased have not lived up to your expectations. Frankly, we are surprised they have proved so fragile and appreciate your returning them to us. Our lab people are already at work trying to discover the source of the problem.

We are glad to assume the shipping costs you incurred, Mr. Patterson. But may we suggest that, instead of a refund, you apply the price of these saws to the cost of an order of model 78b saws. Your own experience will bear out their reliability, and we are sure your customers will be pleased with an Eterna-Tool Product.

If you will drop us a line okaying the shipment, your 78b handsaws will be on their way within the week.

Sincerely yours,

Fig. 6-4

LETTER OF ADJUSTMENT II

REFUSING AN ADJUSTMENT

Like all refusals, this adjustment letter is most difficult to write, for you must try nevertheless to rebuild your customer's goodwill. It must say no graciously but firmly while convincing the customer of the company's fairness and responsibility.

A letter refusing an adjustment should begin by expressing the customer's point of view (see Figure 6-5). It should demonstrate your sympathy and desire to be fair. It should emphasize the careful consideration the claim received.

When saying no, it is often tactful, moreover, to present the explanation *before* the decision and to include an appeal to the customer's sense of fair play. Also, an effective conclusion might suggest an alternative course of action the customer could take.

ATLAS VACUUM CLEANER COMPANY
81 Warren Street
New York, New York 10028

August 28, 19--

Mr. Thomas Shandy
109 Glimmer Circle
Larchmont, New York 10107

Dear Mr. Shandy:

We are sorry that you are not completely satisfied with your Atlas Vacuum Cleaner. You are entirely justified in expecting more than four years of reliable use from an Atlas appliance, and we are always eager to service any product that does not for some reason live up to standard.

We appreciate your giving us the opportunity to examine the damaged vacuum cleaner. According to our service department, the filter had never been replaced although the owner's manual advises replacement every few months. As a result, the motor itself gradually became clogged with dust and dirt.

The cost of repairing and cleaning the vacuum is estimated at $35. If you would like to have it repaired, please let us know. With regular cleaning and replacement of the filter and exhaust bag, you should receive several more years of service from your Atlas appliance.

Yours truly,

Figure 6-5

LETTER OF ADJUSTMENT III

★ PRACTICE CORRESPONDENCE

The situations described in these problems call for either a claim or an adjustment letter. Prepare the appropriate letter as instructed.

A. On June 8, the Venus Hair Salon, 307 Main Street, Middleburg, Virginia 22117, placed an order (no. 6629) for one dozen sets of medium-sized electric rollers with Murphy's Beauty Supplies, Inc., 8022 E. Fourth Street, Richmond, Virginia 22888. The rollers cost $10.95 per set, for a total of $131.40. However, due to a slipup in the shipping department, Murphy's sent one dozen sets of higher-priced jumbo-sized rollers and enclosed an invoice indicating the price as $12.95, for a total of $155.40. Write the claim letter that the Venus Hair Salon should send in order to straighten out the order and receive the rollers they want.

B. Refer to Exercise A and write the adjustment letter that Murphy's Beauty Supplies should send in response. Because of the additional labor and shipping expenses, offer to charge the lower price for the jumbo rollers and encourage the salon to buy another set of medium-sized rollers, also at $10.95 per set.

C. On September 5, Arnold Hayes received a monthly statement from Nayak & Nolan (10 French Market Place, New Orleans, Louisiana 70153), where he has had a charge account for eight years. The statement included a "previous balance" from the August statement. However, Mr. Hayes had promptly paid that balance (of $81.23) on August 7 and has a canceled check to prove it. Write the claim from Mr. Hayes, 80 Arch Drive, New Orleans, Louisiana 70155, asking that his account be cleared up. Mention his enclosure of a check to cover the remaining balance on his account ($107.80).

D. Refer to Exercise C and write the letter of adjustment from Nayak and Nolan, acknowledging the error.

E. On October 7, the Kitchen Korner, 47-03 Parkway Drive, St. Paul, Minnesota 55104, placed an order for two dozen poultry shears from the Northridge Cutlery Company, 2066 Yellow Circle, Minnetonka, Minnesota 55343. By November 30, the shears have still not arrived, and there has been no letter from Northridge Cutlery explaining the delay. Write the claim from Kitchen Korner inquiring about the order. Emphasize these concerns: Did the order arrive? Why was neither an acknowledgment nor a stopgap letter sent? Will the shears arrive in time for pre-Christmas shopping?

F. Refer to Exercise E and write the letter from Northridge Cutlery answering Kitchen Korner's claim. Explain the delay as caused by a strike of local truckers. Apologize for failing to notify the customer.

7.

SALES AND PUBLIC RELATIONS LETTERS

All business letters are in a sense sales letters, as we have already observed. And all business letters are also public relations letters in that one must always seek to establish and maintain goodwill. But some letters are written for the express purpose of selling, and others are written for no other reason than to earn the reader's goodwill.

These letters—*sales* letters and *public relations* letters—require a highly specialized style of writing. Both demand a writer with *flair* and the ability to win the reader with words. For this reason, most large companies employ professional writers—advertising and public relations specialists—who handle all the sales and publicity writing.

Not only do advertising or public relations writers know how to appeal to people's buying motives; they know how to *find* potential buyers. They must know how to acquire mailing lists (such sources as a company's own files, telephone books, and directories are good starts) and how to select the right audience from those lists.

Nevertheless, and especially in smaller companies, there are times when almost any businessperson will have to compose either a sales letter or a public relations letter. While the nuances of style may be beyond the scope of this chapter, certain basic guidelines can help you win a desired sale or earn an associate's goodwill.

Sales Letters

Sales letters may be broken down into three categories: Direct Mail, Retail, and Promotion. While the manner of the sale is different for each, all share a common purpose—to sell a product or service.

DIRECT MAIL SALES LETTERS

Direct mail, or mail order, attempts to sell directly to the customer *through the mail* (Figure 7-1). The direct mail sales letter, therefore, does the entire selling job. A salesperson never calls on the customer; the product is never even seen in person. Solely on the basis of the description and inducements in the letter, the customer is urged to buy—to mail a check and wait for his purchase to arrive.

A direct mail letter must, consequently, include a "hard sell." It must grab the reader's attention with its physical appearance; the use of flashy envelopes and the inclusion of brochures or samples often help. It must

ALL-PRO SPORTING SUPPLIES, INC.
Box 8118
Phoenix, Arizona 85029

March 3, 19--

Dear

What do Miss Universe and Mr. America have in common? They both lift weights to keep in shape--with very different results of course. And many women across the country are discovering--just like Miss Universe--that weight lifting is an effective and fun way to a better-looking body and better health in the bargain.

All-Pro has put together a special package to help women get started. We will send you a pair of three-pound dumbbells and a fully illustrated body-building regime. In just 45 minutes a day, three days a week, these easy-to-follow exercises will firm up every muscle of your body from your deltoids to your calves.

Despite the myths that have grown up around body-building, lifting weights will not make a woman look like a man. Does Farrah Fawcett look like Burt Reynolds? And weight lifting is completely safe. According to Dr. Leonard Paddington of the Phoenix Sports Medicine Institute, "Weight lifting, which strengthens the cardiovascular system, is safe for people of all ages. If you start a weight-lifting program now, you will be able to continue to whatever age you want."

Weight lifting shows results faster than any other form of exercise. Get started now and you'll be all set for your bathing suit and the beach this summer.

Our Women'n'Weights package, with the two dumbbells and complete exercise regime, at the low low price of $21.95, is available only through the mail. You can't buy it in any store. And for a limited time only, we will send you, along with your purchase, an exercise mat FREE. This 100% cotton, quilted mat is machine washable, a $6.96 value.

To order your Women'n'Weights package, and your free exercise mat, SEND NO MONEY NOW. Just fill in the enclosed postage-paid reply card, and your better body will be on its way to you.

Yours truly

Figure 7-1
DIRECT MAIL SALES LETTER

develop the reader's interest with appealing headlines and thorough physical description of the product; several pictures, from different angles, are a good idea.

Moreover, a direct mail letter must convince the reader of the product's quality and value; such evidence as details and statistics, testimonies, and guarantees are essential when a customer cannot see or test a product for herself. And finally, to clinch the deal, a direct mail letter must facilitate action: clear directions for ordering plus a reply card and postage-paid envelope make buying easy; a "send-no-money-now" appeal or the offer of a premium provides additional inducement.

RETAIL SALES LETTERS

Retail sales letters (Figure 7-2) are commonly used by retail businesses to announce sales or stimulate patronage. Their advantage over other forms of advertising (such as television, radio, or newspaper ads) is that letters can be aimed selectively—at the specific audience most likely to buy. An audio shop, for example, holding a sale on telephone-answering equipment, could send letters specifically to local professionals, those customers most apt to need the product.

JUSTIN'S
Winston Salem, NC 27106

January 24, 19--

Dear Customer:

Now that the scaffolds are down and the hammering has stopped, you are probably aware that Justin's has opened a new store in the Bethabara Shopping Center. We are extremely proud of this gleaming new addition to the Justin family.

To celebrate the occasion, we are having a Grand Opening Sale, and every Justin store will be in on it.

EVERYTHING in ALL our stores will be marked down 10–30%. Designer jeans that were $25–$40 are now $20–$36. An assortment of 100% silk blouses, originally $60–$95, are on sale for $40–$65. The savings are incredible.

The sale is for one day only, January 31. But the doors will open at 9 A.M., so you can shop early for the best selection. And, of course, your Justin's and VISA cards are always welcome.

Sincerely yours,

Figure 7-2

RETAIL SALES LETTER

A letter announcing a sale must contain certain information:

1) the reason for the sale (a seasonal clearance, holiday, special purchase, etc.);
2) the dates on which the sale will take place;
3) an honest description of the sale merchandise (including a statement of what is and is not marked down);
4) comparative prices (original price versus sale price or approximate mark-down percentages);
5) a statement encouraging the customer to act fast.

SALES PROMOTION LETTERS

A sales promotion letter (Figure 7-3) solicits interest rather than an immediate sale. It is written to encourage inquiries rather than orders. A product that requires demonstration or elaborate explanation, for example, could be introduced in a promotional letter; interested customers will inquire further. Similarly, products requiring elaborate and expensive descriptive material (for example, a large brochure or sample) could be introduced in a promotional letter; uninterested names on a mailing list would then be screened out, leaving only serious potential customers and thereby cutting costs.

Like other sales letters, a promotional letter must stimulate the reader's interest and describe the product. But it need not be as detailed: customers desiring further information are invited to send in a reply card, contact a sales representative, or visit a local dealer. Of course, such inquiries MUST be answered promptly by either a salesperson or a letter. And the follow-up letter (which could include a leaflet or sample) should provide complete information, including specific answers to questions the customer may have asked. The follow-up must also attempt to convince the reader to buy and tell how to make the purchase.

All of the sales letters described in this chapter have certain features in common: they convey *enthusiasm* for the product and employ *evocative language*. They demonstrate the writer's knowledge of both product and customer. And they illustrate the advertising principles known as AIDA:

1) **A**ttention: The letter opens with a gimmick to grab the reader's attention and create the desire to know more.
2) **I**nterest: The letter provides information and plays up certain features of the product to build the reader's interest.
3) **D**esire: The sales pitch appeals to one or more personal needs (such as prestige, status, comfort, safety, or money) to stimulate the reader's desire.
4) **A**ction: The letter makes it easy for the reader to buy and encourages immediate action.

NEW WAVE STOVE COMPANY
Route 22
Eugene, Oregon 97405

February 10, 19--

Dear

You were right in there when the microwave oven made its debut, and you've seen that "stove of the future" become part of the past, making profits for us both today.

Well, we at New Wave Stove haven't stopped looking toward the future, and we are about to unveil what we expect will be the stove every American housewife will be cooking on by the end of the century--the Sunlight Range.

The Sunlight is a solar-powered stove that uses a set of four reflectors to concentrate the rays of the sun on its cooking chamber. It can do anything a gas or an electric range can do without the high cost of fuels. As Americans become more and more energy conscious, we believe the Sunlight will be the cooking appliance they turn to.

The Sunlight has to be seen to be believed. So we've arranged a week of demonstrations at our factory showroom. To see this solar-powered phenomenon in action, just contact your New Wave representative, _____ , at 824-8229. She'll be happy to arrange an appointment for you.

Yours truly

Figure 7-3

SALES PROMOTION LETTER

Public Relations Letters

Public relations concerns the efforts a company makes to influence public opinion, to create a favorable company image. Its purpose is NOT to make a sale or stimulate immediate business, but rather to convey to the public such positive qualities as the company's reliability, efficiency, or fair-mindedness.

Public relations is big business, and large corporations spend millions of dollars a year on their public relations campaigns. When a major oil company sponsors a program on public television, that is public relations; when a large chemical company establishes a college scholarship fund, that is public relations, too.

The public relations specialist knows how to use all the mass media (television, radio, magazines, newspapers, and films); she knows how to compose press releases and set up press conferences, prepare broadcast announcements, and arrange public receptions.

But public relations exists on a smaller scale as well. It is the local butcher's remembering a shopper's name, and it is the local hardware store buying T-shirts for the Little League. For, basically, public relations is the attempt to establish and maintain GOODWILL.

Public relations letters, therefore, are those letters written for the purpose of strengthening goodwill. Some of these can be considered *social business letters* (see page 77), such as invitations, thank-you notes, and letters of congratulations. Others are akin to advertising, such as announcements of openings or changes in store facilities or policies. Still others are simply friendly gestures, such as a note welcoming a new charge customer or thanking a new customer for her first purchase (Figure 7-4).

PINE & WHITE
100 Massachusetts Avenue
Boston, Massachusetts 02116

June 12, 19--

Ms. Beverly May
100 Gould Street
Needham, Massachusetts 02194

Dear Ms. May:

Now that you've used your Pine & White credit card for the very first time, we are sure you have seen for yourself the convenience and ease a charge account provides. So we won't try to "resell" you on all the benefits you can take advantage of as a new charge customer.

We'd simply like to take this time to thank you for making your first charge purchase and assure you that everyone at Pine & White is always ready to serve you. We are looking forward to a long and mutually rewarding association.

Welcome to the "family."

Sincerely yours,

Ms. Christine Popoulos
Customer Relations

Figure 7-4

PUBLIC RELATIONS LETTER I

A specific kind of public relations letter is designed to demonstrate a company's interest in its customers. This letter (Figure 7-5) is written *inviting* complaints; its purpose is to discover causes of customer dissatisfaction before they get out of hand. (Responses to such letters must always get a prompt follow-up assuring the customer that the reported problem will be looked into.)

PINE & WHITE
100 Massachusetts Avenue
Boston, Massachusetts 02116

May 26, 19--

Mrs. Addison Tanghal
14 East Elm Street
Brookline, Massachusetts 02144

Dear Mrs. Tanghal:

It's been more than six months since you charged a purchase at Pine & White, and we can't help worrying that we've done something to offend you. We are sure you are aware of the convenience and ease your charge account provides, but we would like to assure you once again that everyone at Pine & White is always ready to serve you.

If you have encountered a problem with our service or merchandise, we want to know. It is our sincere desire to give you the personal attention and satisfaction you have come over the years to expect from Pine & White. And we welcome the advice of our customers and friends to keep us on our toes.

Please fill out the enclosed reply card if something has been troubling you. We will give your comments immediate attention, as we look forward to seeing you once again at our Brookline store and all our other branches.

Sincerely,

Ms. Christine Popoulos
Customer Relations

Figure 7-5

PUBLIC RELATIONS LETTER II

Similarly, to forestall complaints (and of course encourage business), large companies frequently send *informative* letters that *educate* the public (Figure 7-6). A supplier of gas and electricity, for example, may include with the monthly bill an explanation of new higher rates. Or a telephone company will enclose a fact sheet on ways to save money on long distance calls.

Whatever the ostensible reason for a public relations letter—to establish, maintain, or even revive business—remember that *all* public relations letters must be *friendly*, for their overriding purpose is to create a friend for the company.

LIQUOR LAND LIQUOR STORES, INC.
Montgomery, Alabama 36044

October 19, 19--

Dear Wine Lover:

Did you know that, in blind tastings among distinguished wine connoisseurs, California wines have been reaping the highest awards for more than the past decade? In fact, California is now recognized internationally as a producer of premium as well as jug wines.

California wines come in three basic types: Varietal wines are named for the grape from which they are made, such as Cabernet Sauvignon, Pinot Noir, and Chardonnay. Generic wines are made in the style of a region elsewhere in the world, such as Burgundy, Port, or Champagne. And Proprietary wines are trademarked according to the name of a wine blend produced by a particular vineyard, such as Wild Irish Rose.

In addition to the better-known vintners, such as Gallo, Almaden, and Paul Masson, California is the home of many small wineries that produce outstanding wine in small quantities. To discover these lesser-known (and often surprisingly affordable) wines is a delight for any wine enthusiast. The perfect place to begin your search is your local Liquor Land, where our friendly wine merchants are eager to recommend their latest finds.

Let us please your palate soon.

Sincerely yours,

Figure 7-6

PUBLIC RELATIONS LETTER III

★ PRACTICE CORRESPONDENCE

On another sheet of paper, prepare either a sales or public relations letter as called for in each of the following situations.

A. Select a product (such as kitchen gadgets, magazines, or cosmetics) that you have considered purchasing (or have actually purchased) by mail. Write a letter that could be used to stimulate direct mail sales for the product.

B. Geoffrey's, a fine men's clothing store located at 10 Arlington Street, Boston, Massachusetts 02116, is having its annual fall clearance sale. All summer and selected fall merchandise will be on sale with discounts up to 60% on some items. The sale will begin on September 10. Write a letter to be sent to all charge customers, inviting them to attend three pre-sale days, September 7–9, during which they will find a full selection of sale merchandise before it is advertised to the public.

C. You work for the ABC Corporation, Fort Madison, Iowa 52622, manufacturer of electric typewriters. Write a letter to be sent to the heads of all business schools in the area, inviting them to inquire about your latest model. Describe some of the typewriter's special features and tell the reader how to receive additional information.

D. You are employed by the First National Bank of Dayton, 1742 Broad Street, Dayton, Ohio 45463. You recently opened both a savings and a checking account for Claire Paulsen, a new resident of Dayton. Write a letter to Ms. Paulsen (222 Elm Street, Dayton, Ohio 45466) to welcome her to the city and to the bank.

E. Imagine that you work in the customer relations department of a large department store. Write a letter that could be sent to charge customers who have not used their accounts in over a year. Remind them of all the advantages, conveniences, and privileges afforded a charge customer and urge them to resume using their accounts.

8.
SOCIAL BUSINESS LETTERS

Like public relations letters, social business correspondence does not promote immediate business. Yet an astute businessperson will recognize the writing of a letter of congratulations or appreciation as a fertile chance to build goodwill.

The occasions that call for social business letters are many; such letters may express congratulations, sympathy, or thanks, or may convey an invitation or announcement. These messages may be extended to friends and personal acquaintances, to co-workers and employees, and to business associates. They may even be sent to persons who are unknown to the writer but who represent potential customers.

While the *tone* of a social business letter will vary with the relationship between the correspondents, all such letters must sound SINCERE. And, with the possible exception of an announcement, they should avoid any hint of a sales pitch.

Social business letters are often written on smaller stationery than letterhead. Some may be handwritten or formally engraved, rather than typed. Moreover, as an additional personalized touch, the salutation in a social business letter may be followed by a comma instead of a colon.

Because the language of a social business letter must strike a delicate balance between the personal and professional, the friendly and formal, it is a good idea to refer to a current book of etiquette for proper wording. Such a reference work will serve as a reliable guide, especially when composing formal invitations and letters of condolence.

Letters of Congratulations

A letter of congratulations builds goodwill by stroking the reader's ego: everyone likes to have accomplishments acknowledged.

The occasions for congratulatory messages are numerous: promotions (Figure 8-1), appointments, and elections; achievements, awards, and honors; marriages and births (Figure 8-2); anniversaries and retirements.

Whether written to a close friend or a distant business associate, any letter of congratulations must be SINCERE and ENTHUSIASTIC. It may be short, but it should contain PERSONAL remarks or references.

A letter of congratulations should contain three essential ingredients; it should:

1) begin with the expression of congratulations;
2) mention the reason for the congratulations with a personal or informal twist;
3) end with an expression of goodwill (such as praise or confidence—NEVER say "Good luck," which implies chance rather than achievement).

Dear Alan,

Congratulations on your promotion to senior accounts executive. You have worked hard for Rembow Consultants, and I am delighted that your efforts have been rewarded.

As you move into your new office and assume the weight of responsibilities that go along with your new position, please let me know if I can be of any assistance.

Sincerely,

Figure 8-1

LETTER OF CONGRATULATIONS I

Dear Monica,

Congratulations on the birth of your grandchild, David Gary. You and Jim must be just thrilled by the experience of becoming grandparents.

Please extend my warmest wishes to your daughter Jane and her husband. May this new addition to your family bring you all great joy.

Sincerely,
Ruth

Figure 8-2

LETTER OF CONGRATULATIONS II

Letters of Sympathy

When an acquaintance experiences the death of a loved one, it is proper, although difficult, to send a message of condolence (see Figures 8-3 and 8-4). To avoid awkwardness, many people opt for commercially printed sympathy cards, but a specially written note is more PERSONAL and GENUINE.

A message of condolence lets your reader know that you are aware of his personal grief and wish to lend sympathy and support. The message, therefore, should be SIMPLE, HONEST, and DIRECT, and it should express SORROW with DIGNITY and RESPECT. (The expression "I am sorry," however, should be avoided, for as a cliché it sounds flat and insincere.)

The message of condolence should begin by referring to the situation and the people involved. This should be a bland statement that avoids unpleasant reminders. The note may use the word *death* but should NOT describe the death.

The rest of the note should be brief: an encouraging reference to the future (which should be uplifting but realistic) or, if appropriate, a gesture of goodwill (such as an offer of help).

Note: A letter of sympathy is also sent to someone who is ill or who has suffered an accident or other misfortune.

Dear Mr. Summers,

I would like to extend the deep sympathy of all of us at Jason Associates.

We had the privilege of knowing and working with Edith for many years, and her friendly presence will be sadly missed.

Please consider us your friends and telephone us if we can be of any help.

Sincerely,

Figure 8-3

LETTER OF CONDOLENCE I

Dear Hal,

Roseann and I were deeply saddened to learn of your great loss. We hope the love you and Edith shared will help comfort you in the days ahead.

If there is anything we can do for you, now or in the future, please let us know.

With much sympathy,

Figure 8-4
LETTER OF CONDOLENCE II

Letters of Appreciation

In business, as in the rest of life, it is important to say "thank you."

We have already seen (see page 33) that letters of appreciation should be sent to new customers upon the opening of an account or the making of a first purchase. But many other occasions call for a "thank you" as well; a note of appreciation should always be sent after receiving:

1) gifts
2) favors
3) courtesies
4) hospitality
5) donations

A note of thanks should also be sent in response to a letter of congratulations.

A thank-you note may be BRIEF, but it must be PROMPT, for it must, like all social business letters, sound SINCERE.

A proper letter of appreciation (see Figures 8-5 and 8-6) will contain three key elements; it will:

1) begin by saying "thank you";
2) make a sincere personal comment;
3) end with a positive and genuine statement. (NEVER say "Thank you again.")

Dear Mr. Houston,

Thank you very much for referring Natalie Slate to us. We are, of course, pleased to take on a new client. But even more, we appreciate your confidence in our legal services and your willingness to communicate this confidence to others.

Be assured that we will continue to make every effort to live up to your expectations.

Cordially,

Figure 8-5

LETTER OF APPRECIATION I

Dear Lucy,

Thank you for the wonderful set of cookbooks. This thoughtful gift helped to make my birthday a very special occasion.

Sincerely,

Figure 8-6

LETTER OF APPRECIATION II

Invitations

While such events as openings, previews, and demonstrations may be advertised in newspapers or on handbills, guests may be more carefully selected if invitations are sent by letter.

Formal events, such as a reception, open house, or formal social gathering, *require* formal invitations. These invitations can be engraved or printed, or they can be handwritten on note-size stationery.

A general invitation (Figure 8-8) should be cordial and sincere; a formal invitation (Figure 8-7) should be less personal, written in the third person. Either kind of invitation, however, must do three things:

1) Invite the reader to the gathering.
2) Give the date, time, and place of the gathering.
3) Offer a reason for the gathering.

A formal invitation should, in addition, include the R.S.V.P. notation. This abbreviation stands for *répondez s'il vous plaît;* it asks the reader to please respond, i.e., "Please let us know if you plan to attend."

THE BROOKDALE CHAMBER OF COMMERCE
requests the pleasure of your company
at a dinner honoring
the Honorable Stacy Coughey
Wednesday, the third of June
at seven o'clock
The Stardust Room of the Excelsior Hotel
R.S.V.P.

Figure 8-7

INVITATION I

JACO FILMS, INC.
1120 Avenue of the Americas
New York, New York 10036

January 3, 19--

Dear

In a few weeks, JACO will proudly release its new feature-length film, The Purchase, starring Amanda Theriot in her first appearance in seventeen years.

A special preview showing of The Purchase, for friends of Ms. Theriot and of JACO Films, will be held on January 19, at 8 P.M., at the Regent Theater on Broadway and 52nd Street.

You are cordially invited to attend this preview. Admission will be by ticket only, which you will find enclosed. Following the film, refreshments will be served.

Sincerely yours,

Figure 8-8

INVITATION II

Announcements

Announcements may rightly be considered closer to public relations than social business letters. They may take the form of news releases, advertisements, or promotional letters. But *formal announcements* resemble invitations in both tone and format. Indeed, the combination formal announcement/invitation (Figure 8-10) is not an uncommon form of correspondence.

Business events such as openings (see Figure 8-9), mergers, and promotions (see Figure 8-11) may be the subject of both formal and informal announcements.

Dr. Richard Levine
announces the opening of his office
for the practice of pediatric medicine
1420 North Grand Street
Suite 1B
Miami, Florida
(402) 889-7626

Figure 8-9

FORMAL ANNOUNCEMENT

The ESCO Corporation
is pleased to announce the appointment of
Ms. Roberta Jenkins
as its new executive vice-president
and requests the pleasure of your company
at a reception in her honor
Friday, the twelfth of April
at four o'clock
The President's Suite   Room 510

Figure 8-10

COMBINATION ANNOUNCEMENT/INVITATION

TO: All Personnel

FROM: George Hart, President

DATE: April 3, 19--

SUBJECT: The New Executive Vice-President

We are pleased to announce the appointment of Ms. Roberta Jenkins to the position of executive vice-president.

Ms. Jenkins has been with ESCO for eight years, first as assistant manager of marketing and then, for the past five years, as manager of marketing. She attended Baruch College and Pace University, where she earned a master's degree in business administration.

I'm sure you will all join me in extending hearty congratulations to Ms. Jenkins and best wishes for her future here at ESCO.

GH

Figure 8-11

INFORMAL ANNOUNCEMENT

★ **PRACTICE CORRESPONDENCE**

For each of the social situations described, prepare a correspondence that is appropriate to business relationships.

A. You are administrative assistant to the president of Burton and Doyle, Inc., 355 Bond Street, Oshkosh, Wisconsin 54901. Your boss, Mr. Arthur J. Burton, asks you to write a letter of congratulations, which he will sign, to Theodore Manning, 72 North Eden, La Crosse, Wisconsin 54601, a junior executive who has just been named "Father of the Year" by the La Crosse Boy Scouts Council.

B. You are employed by American Associates, Inc., 2870 North Howard Street, Philadelphia, Pennsylvania 19122. Your boss, Jacqueline Austin, 450 Poplar Street, Hanover, Pennsylvania 17331, has not been in the office for several days, and it has just been announced that her mother died. Since Ms. Austin will not be returning to work for a week or two, write a letter to express your condolence.

C. You have worked for the law firm of Lederer, Lederer and Hall, 407 East 23 Street, New York, New York 10013, for many years. On the occasion of your tenth anniversary with the company, an office party is held in your honor, and Mr. Gerald Hall presents you with a wristwatch as a token of the company's appreciation. Write a letter to Mr. Hall thanking him and the entire company for the party and the gift.

D. The Merchants Insurance Company of Tucson is holding its annual executive banquet on September 8, 19--, at 7 P.M. It will be held in the Gold Room of the Barclay Country Club, 700 Country Club Road, Tucson, Arizona 85726. Design a *formal* invitation which the company can send to all its executives. Include a request for response by August 24th.

E. A baby, Angela May, has been born to Mr. and Mrs. Andrew Lopato. She was born at Community General Hospital on February 9th at 7 A.M. and weighed seven pounds seven ounces. Prepare a *formal* announcement which the Lopatos could use to inform friends and associates of Angela's birth.

9.
EMPLOYMENT CORRESPONDENCE

Of all the different kinds of letters this book discusses, perhaps none are more important for your personal career than those letters you write to apply for a job. Your letter of application and accompanying resume, if well planned and written, can do much to help you secure the job of your choice.

Before you can write your resume or prepare a cover letter, you must do some thinking about yourself, for your employment correspondence must present a prospective employer with a favorable—and desirable—picture of your personality, background, and experiences.

A good way to start is to make a list. In any order, as you think of them, jot down such facts as:

Schools you have gone to
Areas you have majored in
Special courses you have taken
Extracurricular activities you have joined in
Memberships you have held
Awards or honors you have received
Athletics you enjoy
Languages you speak
Special interests you have
Special skills you have
Jobs you have held

Try to include on your list any FACT that could help an employer see your *value* as an employee.

After you are satisfied with your list, rewrite it, arranging the facts into categories. This will serve as your worksheet when you are ready to write your resume and letter of application.

The Resume

The resume, which is sometimes called a *data sheet* or *vita,* is an OUTLINE of all you have to offer a prospective employer (see Figures 9-1 and 9-2). It is a presentation of your qualifications, your background, and your experiences, arranged in such a way as to convince a businessperson to grant you an interview.

Your resume, with its cover letter, is the first impression you make on an employer. For that reason, it must look PROFESSIONAL and exemplify those traits you want the employer to believe you possess.

Olga Godunov
2500 North Fruitridge Road
Terre Haute, Indiana 47811
(519) 772-1248

CAREER OBJECTIVE:

To obtain a position as an executive secretary with a large
corporation.

WORK EXPERIENCE:

March 1979
to Present

Secretary, the Benlow Corporation, 620 West
Second Street, Terre Haute, Indiana.
Responsible for general running of the office
of a small private firm; duties included typing,
filing, billing, answering telephones,
scheduling appointments, etc.

October 1977
to March 1979

Receptionist, Dr. Mark Roan, 702 South Fulton
Street, Berne, Indiana.

January 1977
to October 1977

File Clerk, Ajax Insurance Company, 277
Westgate Avenue, Berne, Indiana.

EDUCATION:

Judson Secretarial School, Berne, Indiana. September 1976–January
1977. Courses in typing, filing, Gregg shorthand, and business
machines operations.

Central High School, Berne, Indiana. Diploma, June 1976.

SPECIAL SKILLS:

Typing--70 w.p.m.
Shorthand--120 w.p.m.
Languages--French

REFERENCES:

Ms. Alba Jenkins, Owner
The Benlow Corporation
620 West Second Street
Terre Haute, Indiana 47814
(519) 793-8686

Dr. Mark Roan
702 South Fulton Street
Berne, Indiana 46711
(777) 803-9171

Ms. Sarah Cohen, Instructor
Judson Secretarial School
141 River Road
Berne, Indiana 46781

Figure 9-1

RESUME I

Arnold Stevens
25-92 Queens Boulevard
Bayside, New York 11202
(212) 884-7788

Career Objective

An entry-level position in the travel industry

Education

The Bowker Business Institute, 600 Fifth Avenue, New York, New York
10011
    Associate degree, June 1980
    Major: Travel and Tourism
    Courses included: The World of Travel
                      Reservations and Ticketing
                      World Geography
                      Salesmanship
                      Business Management
                      Accounting I
                      Travel Sales and Services
                      Travel Industry Organization

Bayside High School, Bayside, New York
    Diploma, June 1978
    Technical courses included: Typing
                                  Bookkeeping

Work Experience

Sales Assistant   M & M Shoe Store, 70-19 Lefferts Boulevard,
                    Bayside, New York 11202
                    September 1978 to present

Stock Clerk   Same as above
                    September 1977 to September 1978

Skills

Typing: 50 w.p.m.
Language: Spanish

References

References will be furnished on request.

Figure 9-2

RESUME II

       First of all, a resume *must* be TYPED on business-size bond. (It is
acceptable nowadays to send photocopies, but these must be PERFECT
and look like originals. NEVER send a carbon copy!) When your resume is
updated and you add new experiences, you must RETYPE the whole thing.
(*Never* send a resume with handwritten, or even typed, additions squeezed
in. This looks careless, unorganized, and lazy.)

The resume must have an overall NEAT appearance: margins should be wide and balanced. Headings should stand out (for example, be underlined or capitalized) and should be PARALLEL. Corrections should be invisible: the finished product must be PERFECT.

The information contained on your resume must be ACCURATE and COMPLETE. It should consist of FACTS. (You will be able to *interpret* the facts in your application letter.) Because you are presenting these facts in *outline form,* the information should be expressed in short phrases rather than whole sentences.

Nowadays, it is preferable to keep a resume to *one page.* This means that you must be efficient in selecting the facts to include and clever in arranging them.

Working from your casual list, decide which facts you would like an employer to know. (Eliminate those you would rather he not know.) Consider as well what the employer would like to know about you. (Eliminate those facts that he would probably consider irrelevant.)

In making these decisions, keep in mind the specific job for which you are applying. What facts on your list best qualify you for the job? *These* are the facts to emphasize on your resume.

Having narrowed down your list, recopy it again—again arranging the facts into logical order.

Now you are ready to set up your resume. At the top, type your name, address, and telephone number (including your area code). This information can be centered or blocked along the left margin. In either case, it provides a sufficient heading. (The word *resume* is unnecessary.)

The rest of the resume consists of the facts from your list, categorized and typed under headings. Some recommended headings are:

> Employment (or Career) Objective
> Education and/or Training
> Awards and Honors
> Work Experience
> Related or Extracurricular Activities
> Special Skills
> Personal Data
> References

You need not use all of these categories; use, of course, only those that relate to facts on your list. Also, the order in which you list the categories is flexible. You may list your strongest sections first, or you may list first the section that is most relevant to the job in question.

For example, if you have had little business experience but are thoroughly trained, list EDUCATION first. On the other hand, if your college education was in an unrelated field but you have had relevant part-time jobs, list WORK EXPERIENCE first.

Let's look at some of these headings in greater detail:

EMPLOYMENT OBJECTIVE: Many career counselors recommend that this be included and listed first, immediately after your name and address. Mentioning a clearly defined job goal creates the favorable impression that you are a well-directed, motivated individual. On the other hand, many business people now prefer applicants with flexible objectives. Thus, you might consider under this heading a general statement such as, "Acceptance in a management training program" or "Entry-level position in an accounting environment."

EDUCATION: List, in reverse chronological order, the schools you have attended, with names, dates of attendance, and degrees or diplomas awarded. (If you have gone to college, you may omit high school unless your high school experiences are relevant to the job being applied for.) You should list, as well, any job-related courses you have taken. (If you attended a school but did not graduate, include it but be sure to list special courses taken there.)

WORK EXPERIENCE: Between WORK EXPERIENCE and EDUCATION, you must account for *all* your time since high school. (Yes, being a wife and mother for eight years counts as WORK—you've planned and kept a budget, run a household, cared for children—think of the specific responsibilities you have had.) Part-time and summer jobs count here, too, as does volunteer work. (You needn't have gotten paid to have developed a valuable and marketable skill.)

Each job experience should be listed (again, with the most recent job first) with your position or title, employer's name and address (and preferably telephone number), dates of employment, and a brief description of your responsibilities.

Note: If you have been in the armed services, this may be included under WORK EXPERIENCE or a separate heading. Be sure to list the branch of the military, dates, special duties, and highest rank held.

EXTRACURRICULAR ACTIVITIES and SPECIAL SKILLS: Under these headings you may list any facts that don't fit under EDUCATION or WORK EXPERIENCE but which demonstrate an important aspect of your value to an employer. For example, if you can type and take dictation but have never held a secretarial position, here is where to list your speeds. If you can operate specialized machinery or speak a foreign language, note these facts as well.

Similarly, if you were treasurer of an after-school club, your experience handling money and specific duties that you performed are all important to mention. Indeed, all such memberships and activities are worth noting, for they help draw a picture of a vital, well-rounded individual.

PERSONAL DATA: It is not necessary to list such facts as age, height, weight, health, and marital status. Indeed, FEDERAL and many STATE LAWS prohibit employers from asking about race, religion, or sex. So some career counselors advise omitting this category altogether.

However, if a personal fact is particularly relevant to the job you are seeking, it may be worth mentioning (though using a heading such as MISCELLANEOUS may be better than PERSONAL DATA). For example, having a family member employed in the field could indicate that you have a thorough understanding of the responsibilities, as well as advantages and disadvantages, of the job. Or, being in perfect health could be important on a job that requires a great deal of physical activity or even long or irregular hours.

REFERENCES: The *last* section of your resume is a list of those people willing to vouch for your ability and experience. Former employers and teachers (especially teachers of job-related courses) are the best references. Friends or members of the clergy may be used as *character* references, but their word regarding your skills will have little weight.

Each reference should be listed by name, position or title, business address, and telephone number. A minimum of three names is recommended. Alternatively, under this heading, you may simply state, "References furnished on request," if you prefer to give a prospective employer photostated copies of previously prepared letters of reference.

Note: Be sure to ask permission of each individual before you list anyone as a reference. Also, while some employers prefer to contact your references directly, it is a good idea to get a general letter of reference from each to keep for your own files. (Businesses move or go bankrupt; people move, retire, or die; and, after many years, you may simply have been forgotten!)

Letters of Application

A *letter of application* is a *sales letter* in which you are both salesperson and product, for the purpose of a letter of application is to *attract* an employer's attention and *persuade* her to grant you an interview. To do this, the letter presents what you can offer the employer, rather than what you want from the job.

Like a resume, the letter of application is a *sample of your work;* and it is, as well, an opportunity to *demonstrate,* not just talk about, your skills and personality. If it is written with flair and understanding and prepared with professional care, it is likely to hit its mark.

There are two types of application letters. A SOLICITED letter is sent in response to a help-wanted ad (see, for example, Figure 9-3). Because such a letter will be in competition with many, perhaps several hundred, others, it must be composed with distinction. At the same time, it must refer to the ad and the specific job advertised.

An UNSOLICITED letter (Figure 9-4) is sent to a company for which you would like to work though you know of no particular opening. The advantage of this type of application, however, is that there will be little competition and you can define yourself the position you would like to apply for. Too, you can send out as many of these letters as you wish, to as many companies as you are aware of; it is a good idea, though, to find out the name of a specific person to whom you can send the letter—a more effective approach than simply addressing a letter to "Personnel."

Every letter of application must be *originally typed.* Indeed, each one should be freshly composed to suit the particular job or company it is seeking. It must *never* be typed on letterhead or personal stationery, but on plain business-size bond. Like the resume, it must be *perfect,* and it should serve, moreover, as a proof that you have mastered the principles of business correspondence.

Because a letter of application must sell your qualifications, it must do more than simply restate your resume in paragraph form. While the resume must be factual, objective, and brief, the letter is your chance to interpret and expand. It should state explicitly how your background relates to the specific job, and it should emphasize your strongest and most pertinent characteristics. The letter should demonstrate that you know both yourself and the company.

2500 North Fruitridge Road
Terre Haute, Indiana 47811
March 1, 19--

Mr. John P. Storm, Vice-President
Indiana Gas and Electric Company
1114 Broad Street
Terre Haute, Indiana 47815

Dear Mr. Storm:

Having served for the past several years as the sole secretary of a
private business, I would like to apply for the position of executive
secretary which you advertised in the Terre Haute Gazette of Sunday,
February 28, 19--.

As secretary to the Benlow Corporation here in Terre Haute, I was
directly responsible to Ms. Alba Jenkins, the company's owner. My
services were generally those of a "gal Friday." In addition to the
usual typing, filing, and taking dictation, I was responsible for scheduling all of Ms. Jenkins' appointments, screening her telephone calls
and visitors, and organizing her paperwork and correspondence.

Essentially, I did everything I could to make Ms. Jenkins' heavy responsibilities easier. Thus, I am familiar with the duties of an executive secretary and believe I am prepared to anticipate and meet all
your expectations. I am confident, too, that, with enthusiasm and
sincere effort, I can make the transition from a small business to a
large corporation smoothly.

I would appreciate your giving me the opportunity to discuss my qualifications in person. I would be happy to come for an interview at your
convenience, and I can be reached after 5 P.M. at 772-1248.

Sincerely yours,

Figure 9-3

LETTER OF APPLICATION I

A letter of application must communicate your ambition and enthusiasm. Yet it must, at the same time, be *modest*. It should be neither aggres-
sive nor meek: neither pat yourself on the back nor ask for sympathy. It
should *never* express dissatisfaction with a present or former job or employer. And you should avoid discussing your reasons for leaving your last
job. (If asked this question at an interview, your answer, though honest,
should be positive and favorable.)

25-92 Queens Boulevard
Bayside, New York 11202
June 15, 1980

Ms. Loretta Vasquez
The Vasquez Travel Agency
1402 Broadway
New York, New York 10032

Dear Ms. Vasquez:

This month I completed a two-year course of study in Travel and
Tourism at the Bowker Business Institute, and my placement counselor,
Mr. Robert Feiner, suggested I apply to you for a position as assistant
travel agent.

As you will see from my enclosed resume, I have taken courses in
nearly every aspect of the travel industry. I have participated in work-
shops simulating computer and telephone operations, and I have had
extensive practice in ticketing and reservations.

My work experience, moreover, has helped me develop an ability to
deal with the public, a valuable asset for a travel agency. Not only as
a sales assistant, but even as a stock clerk, I have learned to be customer oriented; I have found that courtesy and a smile keep business
flowing smoothly.

I would like very much, Ms. Vasquez, to put my skills to work for your
travel agency. I am available for an interview Monday through Friday
during business hours. You can reach me at 884-7788.

Yours truly,

Figure 9-4

LETTER OF APPLICATION II

When you begin to write your letter of application, keep in mind the principles of writing sales letters:

1) *Start by attracting attention.* You must say, of course, that you are applying and mention both the specific job and how you heard about it (or, in an unsolicited letter, why you are interested in the particular company). But try to avoid a mundane opening. Instead of:

> I would like to apply for the position of legal secretary which you advertised in the *Los Angeles Times* of Sunday, August 10, 19--.

try something a *bit* more original:

> I believe you will find that my experiences in the Alameda District Attorney's office have prepared me well for the position of legal secretary which you advertised in the *Los Angeles Times* of Sunday, August 10, 19--.

2) *Continue by describing your qualifications.* Highlight your strengths and achievements and *say* how they suit you for the job at hand. Provide details and explanations (even brief anecdotes) not found on your resume, and refer the reader to the resume for the remaining, less pertinent facts.

3) *Assure the employer that you are the person for the job.* List verifiable facts that prove you are not exaggerating or lying. Mention the names of any familiar or prominent references you may have. In some way distinguish yourself from the mass of other qualified applicants.

4) *Conclude by requesting an interview.* Without being coercive, urge the employer to action by making it easy to contact you. Mention your telephone number (even though it is on your resume) and the best hours to reach you. Or, mention that you will call him within a few days. (Keep in mind that, while some employers will consider a follow-up call admirably ambitious, others will consider it pushy and annoying. Use your judgment.)

A complete application should contain both a letter of application and a resume. While it is possible to write a letter so complete in detail that a resume seems redundant, it is always most professional to include both.

It is best NOT to include copies of your letters of reference or of your school transcripts. These can be provided later if you are granted an interview. In a similar vein, do not include a photograph of yourself. The briefer the original application, the better.

A final word about salary: basically, unless instructed by the want ad, it is best that you not broach the subject. Indeed, even if an ad requires that you mention your salary requirements, it is advisable simply to call them "negotiable." However, when you go on an interview, you should be prepared to mention a salary range (e.g., $10,000–$12,000). For this reason, you should investigate both your field and, if possible, the particular company. You don't want to ask for less than you deserve or more than is reasonable.

Follow-Up Letters   Few people nowadays send a *follow-up letter* (Figure 9-5) after an interview. For this reason alone, it can be highly effective.

A follow-up letter should be *courteous* and *brief*. It should merely thank the employer for the interview and restate your interest in the job. A reference to a successful moment at the interview is a good, personalizing touch.

25-92 Queens Boulevard
Bayside, New York 11202
June 25, 1980

Ms. Loretta Vasquez
The Vasquez Travel Agency
1402 Broadway
New York, New York 10032

Dear Ms. Vasquez:

Thank you for allowing me to discuss my travel qualifications in person.

Having met you and Mrs. DeLoia, and seen your agency in operation, I sincerely hope I will have the chance to put my training to work for you.

Enclosed is a copy of my transcript from the Bowker Business Institute, along with the letters of reference you requested. I can be reached at 884-7788 during regular business hours.

Sincerely yours,

Figure 9-5

FOLLOW-UP LETTER

Letters of Reference and Recommendation

The difference between letters of reference and recommendation is slim. A *recommendation* (Figure 9-7) is an endorsement while *a reference* (Figure 9-6) is simply a report. A recommendation is persuasive while a reference verifies facts.

Both types of letters start out the same. Each should include:

1) a statement of the letter's purpose;
2) an account of the duties performed by the applicant or of the applicant's general qualifications.

A letter of recommendation would add a third item—a concluding statement specifically *recommending* the applicant for the particular position.

Note: When writing a reference or recommendation, it is advisable to mark both the envelope and letter "Confidential" to protect both yourself and the applicant.

M & M SHOE STORE
70-19 Lefferts Boulevard
Bayside, New York 11202

June 17, 1980

Ms. Loretta Vasquez
The Vasquez Travel Agency
1402 Broadway
New York, New York 10032

Dear Ms. Vasquez:

I am happy to provide the information you requested regarding Arnold Stevens, with the understanding that this information will be kept confidential.

Mr. Stevens has been a stock clerk and then sales assistant in my store since September 1977. He has always been willing to work odd hours, including weekends and holidays, and has proven to be a hard-working and trustworthy employee.

Sincerely yours,

Otto Munson
Proprietor

Figure 9-6

LETTER OF REFERENCE

THE BOWKER BUSINESS INSTITUTE
600 Fifth Avenue
New York, New York 10011

June 17, 1980

Ms. Loretta Vasquez
The Vasquez Travel Agency
1402 Broadway
New York, New York 10032

Dear Ms. Vasquez:

Arnold Stevens was a student in three of my travel courses since the Fall 1978 semester. He was always an outstanding student.

Mr. Stevens demonstrated his thorough grasp of the subject matter in his class performance as well as written work. His assignments were always executed with conscientiousness and punctuality. Moreover, he was an enthusiastic participant in class discussions and helped to make the courses rewarding experiences for everyone else involved.

Therefore, I can recommend Mr. Stevens, without hesitation, for the position of assistant in your travel agency.

Yours truly,

Jack Adler
Instructor

Figure 9-7
LETTER OF RECOMMENDATION

Letters of Introduction

Rather different from but not entirely unrelated to employment letters are *letters of introduction* (Figure 9-8). These are written to a business associate on behalf of a third person (such as an employee, customer, or client). Such a letter is written when one person you know would like to establish a business relationship with another person whom you also know but whom he himself does not.

The letter of introduction you would write in such a situation should include three points:

1) the relationship between you and the person being "introduced";
2) your reason for introducing him to your reader;
3) what you (or he) would like the reader to do for him.

The letter of introduction is sort of a cross between a request and a reference. It should be worded with *courtesy*.

Generally, the letter of introduction is given to the individual being introduced, who in turn delivers it in person. However, it is customary to forward a copy of the letter, along with an explanatory (and less formal) cover letter, so that your reader will anticipate the visit.

THE VASQUEZ TRAVEL AGENCY
1402 Broadway
New York, New York 10032

May 20, 1981

Mr. Jonathan Vecchio
Alpine Leisure Village
Aurora, Colorado 80707

Dear Jonathan:

Arnold Stevens has been my assistant for the past year, and he is currently touring the Denver-Aurora area.

So that he may knowledgeably inform our clients of the many delights of Alpine Leisure Village, I would greatly appreciate your giving him a tour of your facilities when he visits.

With much appreciation,

Loretta Vasquez

Figure 9-8

LETTER OF INTRODUCTION

★ PRACTICE CORRESPONDENCE

Prepare your own employment correspondence according to the following instructions.

A. List all the facts you can think of about your personality, background, and experiences. Then arrange the list in a logical order and decide on categories under which to group the facts. From this worksheet, prepare your resume.

B. Imagine the ideal job for which you would like to apply. With this job in mind, write an unsolicited letter of application to a prospective employer and ask for an interview.

C. Prepare a letter of application answering the following classified advertisement.

OFFICE ASST

Textile distributor has highly diversified position for person who enjoys detailed work & has good typing. Business background helpful. $200/wk. Box 7705

10.
IN-HOUSE CORRESPONDENCE

The letters discussed so far were, for the most part, intended to be sent to people outside one's own company. Messages to customers, clients, and other business associates, they placed heavy emphasis on business promotion and goodwill. But business people frequently must communicate in writing with employees of their own company. The primary purpose of *in-house correspondence* is to share information.

The Interoffice Memorandum

Memorandums, more usually called *memos,* are the form commonly used for *short,* relatively *informal* messages between members of the same organization (see Figure 10-1). The memo provides a simplified, standardized format for communicating information *concisely.* The many uses of memos include announcements and instructions, statements of policy, and informal reports.

Because memos are usually used between people who have a regular working relationship, the *tone* of memos tends to be more informal than the tone of other business letters. Company jargon, for example, is permissible in a memo. Similarly, the writer can usually assume that the reader knows the basic facts and so can get to the heart of the message with little buildup. Note, however, that the level of formality should reflect the relationship between the writer and the reader.

At the same time, a memo, like any piece of written communication, must be prepared with care. It must be TYPED neatly and contain COMPLETE, ACCURATE information. It should adhere to the principles of standard English and maintain a COURTEOUS tone no matter how familiar the correspondents may be.

Unlike other types of business letters, the memo is NOT prepared on company letterhead. Nor does it include an inside address, salutation, or complimentary closing. A memo is a streamlined form and, indeed, many companies provide printed forms to speed up memo preparation even further.

Whether or not a printed form is provided, most memos use a standard heading: the company name about one inch from the top followed by the term "Interoffice Memo." Beneath this, four basic subheadings are used:

TO:
FROM:
DATE:
SUBJECT:

C. P. DALLOWAY & SONS
Interoffice Memo

TO: Charles Dalloway, Jr.

FROM: Clarissa Woolf

DATE: August 18, 19--

SUBJECT: Search for a New Secretary for the Legal Department

Here is the progress report you requested about our search for a new secretary.

We have now interviewed eight individuals and have narrowed our choices to three:

1 Margaret O'Connell--types 65 w.p.m., takes dictation at 120 w.p.m., has had five years' experience in a law office.

2 Daisy Robinson--types 70 w.p.m., takes dictation at 120 w.p.m., has just graduated from Providence Community College (majoring in Secretarial Studies).

3 Donald Trumbo--types 65 w.p.m., takes dictation at 100 w.p.m., has worked as a legal assistant for three years and taken paralegal courses at Providence Community College.

Members of the Legal Department will meet tomorrow, August 19, at 9:30 A.M., to discuss the candidates and make a decision. Your presence at the meeting (in Ms. Gray's office) is, of course, welcome.

CW

Figure 10-1

INTEROFFICE MEMORANDUM

(Some companies also include space for such details as office numbers or telephone extensions.)

The TO: line indicates the name of the person to whom the memo is sent. Courtesy titles (such as *Mr.* or *Ms.*) are generally used only to show respect to a superior; job titles, departments, and room numbers may be included to avoid confusion. When several people will be receiving copies, a CC notation may be added or an inclusive term used (such as "TO: All Personnel").

The FROM: line indicates the name of the person sending the memo. No courtesy title should be used, but a job title, department, or extension number may be included for clarity or convenience.

The DATE: line indicates in standard form the date on which the memo is sent.

The SUBJECT: line serves as a title and so should briefly but thoroughly describe the content of the memo.

The body of the memo begins three to four lines below the subject line. Like any piece of writing, it should be logically organized. But it should also be CONCISE: the information should be immediately accessible to the reader. For this reason, data are often itemized in memos and paragraphs are numbered. Too, statistics should be presented in tables.

The body of most memos can be divided into three general sections:

An introduction states the main idea or purpose.
A detailed discussion presents the actual information being conveyed.
A conclusion may make recommendations or call for further action.

Note: Memos are not usually signed. The writer's initials are typed below the message, and if she chooses she may sign her initials over the typed ones or at the FROM line. Reference initials and enclosure notation are typed below the writer's initials along the left margin.

Minutes

Within most organizations, meetings among members of departments or committees are a regular occurrence. Some meetings are held at fixed intervals (such as weekly or monthly) and others are called for special reasons. *Minutes* (Figure 10-2) are a written record of everything that transpires at a meeting. They are prepared for the company files, for the reference of those in attendance, and for the information of absentees.

Minutes are prepared by a secretary who takes thorough notes during the proceedings. Afterwards, she prepares a *draft* and includes all the pertinent information. (It is usually the secretary's responsibility to decide which statements or actions at a meeting are insignificant and so should be omitted from the minutes.)

In preparing the minutes, the secretary may include complete versions of statements and papers read at the meeting. (Copies are provided by the member involved.) The minutes of *formal* meetings (of, for example, large corporations or government agencies), where legal considerations are involved, are made *verbatim.* That is, they include, word for word, everything that is said or done.

The format used for minutes varies from one organization to another. But the minutes of any meeting should contain certain basic facts:

1) the name of the organization;
2) the place, date, and time of the meeting;
3) whether the meeting is regular (monthly, special, etc.);
4) the name of the person presiding;
5) a record of attendance (for small meetings, a list of those present or absent; for large meetings, the number of members in attendance);
6) a reference to the minutes of the previous meeting (a statement that they were read and either accepted or revised, or that the reading was dispensed with);
7) an account of all reports, motions, or resolutions made (including all necessary details and the results of votes taken);
8) the date, time, and place of the next meeting;
9) the time of adjournment.

Formal minutes would include, in addition to greater detail, the names of all those who make and second motions and resolutions, and the voting record of each person present.

Minutes of the Meeting of the
CAPITOL IMPROVEMENTS COMMITTEE
The Foster Lash Company, Inc.
October 8, 19--

Presiding: Patricia Stuart

Present: Jay Townes
        Sheila Gluck
        Ellen Franklin
        Samuel Browne
        Lisa Woo

Absent: Fred Hoffman
      Gina Marino

The weekly meeting of the Capitol Improvements Committee of the Foster Lash Company was called to order at 11 A.M. in the conference room by Ms. Stuart. The minutes of the meeting of October 1 were read by Mr. Townes and approved.

The main discussion of the meeting concerned major equipment that should be purchased by the end of the year. Among the proposals were these:

Ms. Woo presented information regarding three varieties of office copying machines. On the basis of her cost analysis and relative performance statistics, it was decided, by majority vote, to recommend the purchase of a CBM X-12 copier.

Mr. Browne presented a request from the secretarial staff for new typewriters. Several secretaries have complained of major and frequent breakdowns of their old machines. Ms. Franklin and Mr. Browne are to further investigate the need for new typewriters and prepare a cost comparison of new equipment versus repairs.

The committee will discuss the advisability of purchasing a small in-house computer; the report will be presented by Sheila Gluck at the next meeting, to be held on October 15, 19--, at 11 A.M. in the conference room.

The meeting adjourned at 11:45 A.M.

Respectfully submitted,

Ellen Franklin, Secretary

Figure 10-2
MINUTES

★ PRACTICE CORRESPONDENCE

Prepare the in-house correspondence called for in each of the following situations.

A. Your employer, Penelope Louden, requested a schedule of the data processors' planned vacations so that she may decide whether or not to arrange for temporary help during the summer months. The schedule is as follows: Josie Thompkins, July 1–15; Calvin Bell, July 15–29; Stephen James, July 22–August 5; Jennifer Coles, August 12–26. Prepare a memo to Ms. Louden informing her of the schedule and observing that at least three processors will always be present—except during the week of July 22, when both Mr. Bell and Mr. James will be on vacation. Ask if she'd like you to arrange for a temporary processor for that week.

B. As administrative assistant to the president of Conway Products, Inc., it is your responsibility to make reservations at a local restaurant for the annual Christmas party. Because of the high cost per person, you would like to have as accurate a guest list as possible. Therefore, write a memo to all the employees requesting that they let you know by December 1 whether they plan to attend.

C. As secretary to the Labor Grievances Committee of the Slate and Johnson Luggage Company, you must prepare the minutes of the monthly meeting held on September 23. At the meeting, you took the following notes:

1. Called to order 4 P.M., employees' cafeteria, by Mr. Falk.

2. Presiding: Mr. Falk; Present: Mr. Baum, Ms. Dulugatz, Mr. Fenster, Ms. Garcia, Ms. Penn; Absent: Mr. Sun.

3. Correction made in minutes of previous meeting (August 21): Ms. Dulugatz, not Ms. Penn, to conduct study of employee washroom in the warehouse. Approved as corrected.

4. Mr. Fenster presented results of survey of office employees. Most frequent complaints agreed on. Fenster to arrange to present these complaints to Board of Directors.

5. Report on condition of warehouse employee washrooms presented by Ms. Dulugatz. Accepted with editorial revision.

6. Adjourned 5:15 P.M. Next meeting at same time and place on October 22.

D. As secretary to the Highridge Tenants Association, prepare minutes from the following notes taken at the emergency meeting on May 4, 19--:

1. Called to order 7:30 P.M. lobby, by Ms. Gingold.

2. 102 members present, 13 absent, all officers present.

3. Reading of minutes of last meeting dispensed with.

4. Officers' Reports—
Vice-President read through the "red herring" sent by landlord to tenants. Explained more difficult clauses. Explained lengthy court procedure before actual cooperative offering can be made.
Treasurer reported balance of $87.10. Observed need for minimum of $500 to retain an attorney to negotiate with landlord. Requested members with unpaid dues to see him after meeting.

5. Motions—
    The President called for a committee to search for a lawyer to represent tenants. Motion made and carried that floor captains will constitute the committee headed by the President.
    Motion to meet again to vote on search committee's selection made and carried.

6. Adjourned 9:30 P.M.

11.
TELEGRAMS

Telegrams are still a common means of transmitting messages when delay must be avoided—despite the latest advances in telecommunications and information processing. Of the various forms of telegrams, Western Union telegrams are the fastest but most expensive; other choices include night telegrams and mailgrams. The class of service you choose will depend upon such factors as the length of your message and the time of day it is sent.

Regular telegrams are transmitted immediately at any time of day or night—usually by telephone although delivery in writing can be arranged at an extra charge. The cost is based on a 15-word minimum, with extra charge for each additional word.

When a telegram would arrive after a business has closed for the day, an economical alternative is a night telegram. This can be sent any time until midnight, for delivery the following morning. Night telegrams are less expensive than regular telegrams, with the standard rate usually based on a 100-word minimum with an additional charge for each word over 100.

Mailgrams employ a combination of telegraph and postal services. They are less expensive than either regular or night telegrams; their minimum cost is based on the first 100 words with extra charge for each additional group of 100 words. They can be sent any time until 7 P.M. by calling Western Union to dictate the message, which is automatically transferred to the post office, printed out, and delivered with the following day's mail. (Some companies are equipped with such machines as telex to transmit their own mailgrams.)

Because the cost of telegrams is based on word count, they must be kept BRIEF and CONCISE. They should be used to convey only *vital information,* not explanatory material or data already understood by both sender and reader. They must be free of redundancy and all *unnecessary words* (that is, words which could be omitted without blurring the meaning).

While complete sentences are not necessary in a telegram, the idea is to condense the word count without affecting the CLARITY or COMPLETENESS of the message. Thus, short words such as articles and conjunctions may be left out, but only if the meaning remains·comprehensible.

The basic technique when preparing a message for a telegram is to list the facts and then delete and condense until only the bare essentials remain. (Of course, when you are finished, reread your message carefully to be sure you have conveyed your meaning clearly.)

For example, to make hotel reservations, you could send the following letter:

> Dear Sirs:
>
> I will be attending the American Philatelists' Convention during the week of June 29, 19--, and would like to reserve a two-room suite with bath. I will arrive in Fordham at approximately 4 P.M. on June 29 and will be staying for five days.
>
> I would appreciate your confirming this reservation.
>
> Sincerely yours,

Such a message, however, would be much too costly to send by telegram and would have to be simplified:

> Reserve 2-room suite bath June 29 to July 3. Arriving 4 P.M. Confirm.

By keeping the message to 15 words, the speed of a telegram remains economical.

Night telegrams or mailgrams, on the other hand, allow more leeway —at 100 words they can include more detail and still reach their destination quickly. A mailgram would be suitable, for example, for sending specifications to a customer who needs information in a hurry. Consider the following catalog description:

> SUBZERO PARKA is one of our warmest down parkas, suitable for severe conditions because of its rugged and extremely warm triple-layer construction. It is made of 9.5 ounces of high-quality 550 fill-power goose down quilted to an inner shell of 2.2-ounce nylon taffeta. The outer shell of 65% polyester/35% cotton is wind and water resistant. Because down "breathes," it is comfortable over a wide range of temperatures.
>
> Lightweight and well designed, the jacket has a 32"-long body, adjustable drawstring waist, down-filled collar, and adjustable cuffs. Its raglan shoulders allow freedom of movement; the nylon coil zipper is covered by an insulated flap that prevents drafts. It has two hand-warmer/cargo pockets and a zipper-closing map pocket on the outside and another zipper pocket on the inside.
>
> The parka weighs about 3 pounds and may be dry-cleaned or hand-washed and drip-dried. Men's sizes only: XSm (30–32), Sm (34–36), Med (38–40), Lg (42–44), XLg (46–48).
>
> 144M SUBZERO PARKA, $148.00 ppd.

Rather than send an entire catalog by regular mail, you could condense this description to 100 words and, by mailgram, get it to your customer by the next day:

SUBZERO PARKA is one of our warmest, suitable for severe conditions, comfortable over wide range of temperatures, wind and water resistant. Rugged, warm triple layer construction: 9.5 ounces high quality 550 fill power goose down quilted to inner shell of 2.2 ounce nylon taffeta, outer shell 65% polyester, 35% cotton. Has 32″ long body, adjustable cuffs, raglan shoulders, insulated flap over zipper, 4 pockets. Weighs 3 pounds. Dry clean or hand wash. Men's sizes only: XSm (30–32), Sm (34–36), Med (38–40), Lg (42–44), XLg (46–48).

144M SUBZERO PARKA, $148 ppd.

Can ship immediately.

When preparing a telegram form, type the message in regular letter format. (Omit the salutation and complimentary closing, however.) You may single space if the message is long, double space if short. Indicate all paragraph breaks clearly.

DO NOT type the message in all capital letters. Use regular punctuation marks, for which there is no charge. (Avoid the archaic STOP, for example, for it is charged as a word whereas a period is free.) Avoid abbreviations and contractions (they are charged as words anyway), and do not divide words at the end of lines.

Be sure, too, to provide all the information requested on the form (page 270):

1) class of service (i.e., regular or night telegram);
2) company name (to be charged to);
3) payment method ("Pd." if prepaid, "Coll." if receiver will pay);
4) inside address, including telephone number, ZIP code, and date—at top;
5) sender's name, address, and telephone number—at bottom.

Be sure, as well, to type the sender's signature and company name two lines below the message.

As you compose your telegrams, keep in mind these guidelines regarding chargeable words:

1) There is no charge for the inside address, date, and signature, or for punctuation.
2) Numbers should be transmitted in figures, not words *(22,* not *twenty-two).* Figures and letters in a sequence are charged as one word for every five characters. *(10463,* for instance, is one word, while *284-IXF* is two words.)
3) Spaced initials are charged as separate words, but typed without spaces initials are charged as one word for every five letters. (Similarly, name prefixes count as extra words when separated from the name by a space: *Du Pont* counts as two words whereas *McGuire* counts as one.)
4) Each word of a place name is counted separately. (*New Jersey,* therefore, is counted as two words. *NJ,* though, would count as one.)

5) Abbreviations of single words count as whole words.
6) Some symbols cannot be transmitted and must be indicated by word: ¢ (cent), @ (at), ° (degree). Other symbols may be used: $, #, &, /, ' (feet), " (inches); these symbols are charged as one word unless part of an unbroken sequence of five characters (see #2 above). *Percent* may be transmitted as *o/o* and is counted as three characters in a sequence.

NO.WDS.–CL. of SVC.	PD. or COLL.	CASH NO.	CHARGE TO THE ACCOUNT OF	☐ OVERNIGHT TELEGRAM
				Unless box above is checked this message will be sent as a telegram.

Send the following message

TO   CARE OF
                                                        or APT. NO.

STREET & NO.

                                                        TELEPHONE

CITY & STATE

                                                        ZIP CODE

Sender's Tel. No.   Name & Address

Figure 11-1

TELEGRAM FORM

★ PRACTICE CORRESPONDENCE

On another sheet of paper, prepare an economical telegram for each of the following situations.

A. You will be visiting an old friend in Chicago for a few days. Prepare a telegram informing her that you will be arriving at O'Hare International Airport on Trans World Airlines flight 772 on Tuesday, March 3, at 11 in the morning.

B. Revise the following letter so that it may be sent as a telegram:

Dear Sirs:

Our Purchase Order 8033, dated April 9, 19--, for three dozen pairs of gardener's gloves, has not yet arrived.

If the order has not already been shipped, we would like it sent air express because our stock of gloves is nearly depleted.

Yours truly,

C. Your employer, Benjamin Da Silva, assistant vice-president of the Sierra Tractor Company, is on vacation at the Paradise Inn, Miami, Florida 33494. Suddenly, a wildcat strike is called by employees of the assembly plant in Ronkonkoma. Company president Lena Postikian has requested all executives and managers to attend an emergency meeting at 9 A.M. tomorrow morning. Prepare a telegram to Mr. Da Silva informing him of the strike and the meeting.

D. You are employed by Northeast Conservation Products, Inc., 16 West Tenth Street, Somersworth, New Hampshire 03878. You have received a telegram from a regular customer, Joe Arnell of Arnell's Contractors and Builders, Inc., 1213 Locust Street, Des Moines, Iowa 50331, requesting specifications regarding chimney dampers suitable for an old home that is being renovated. Using the following catalog description, prepare a night telegram that will give Mr. Arnell the information he needs.

CHIMNEY TOP DAMPER If you live in an old house with no damper in the fireplace, or even in a new house whose damper may have become warped by intense heat and so no longer seals properly, you are wasting precious energy and money as the heat goes up and out. Installed at the TOP of your chimney, our cast aluminum damper seals against extensive heat loss and prevents entry of birds, squirrels, and insects as well as rain and snow. Moreover, since warm air remains inside the chimney, your fireplace will draw immediately, and not smoke, when you light a fire.

The damper is instantly opened or closed by a stainless steel cable which drops down inside the chimney to a bracket mounted to a forward part of the fireplace wall. Spring loading keeps the damper open normally; it cannot accidentally close when a fire is going. It is designed for standard terra cotta flue tiles or chimney openings, with outside dimensions of 9" × 13", 13" × 13", or 13" × 18". Please measure carefully before ordering.
P-6999 $75.55

12.
NEWS RELEASES

A *news release* is a form of publicity writing. It is usually an announcement of an event or development within a company. Such occurrences as meetings, appointments, promotions, and expansions, as well as the introduction of new products or services and the dissemination of financial information, are all potential subjects for news releases.

News releases are sent to company publications and the mass media (specifically newspapers, radio, and television) in the hope that the editor will approve the release for publication or broadcast. In order to be accepted by an editor, therefore, a release must do more than promote a company's image and goodwill; it must be NEWSWORTHY and TIMELY. That is, it must interest the audience.

Like memos and minutes, news releases do not use standard business letter format. Nor do they use the *"you*-oriented" tone of voice referred to so often in this book. Both the layout and language of a news release are aimed at making it "copy ready." The less rewriting a release requires, the more likely an editor will be to accept it.

A news release should be *concise* and *straightforward;* it should contain no superfluous words. Nor should it contain confusing words: its meaning should be easily understood. Moreover, it should be written in an impersonal style. Your company, for example, should be referred to by name, not as "our company" or "we." Individuals, including oneself, should similarly be referred to by name—almost as if an outsider or reporter had written the story. References to dates and times, as well, should be specific. (Words like *today, tomorrow,* and *yesterday* are pointless when you can't be sure when your release will see print.)

The first, or lead, paragraph of a news release is the most important. Since an editor, if space is needed for a more newsworthy item, may chop away parts of your release from the bottom up, the lead paragraph should be capable of standing on its own. It should summarize the event and contain all the essential details. Following paragraphs should elaborate with additional information in order of importance. As in all business writing, ACCURACY and COMPLETENESS of details are essential; but in a news release even a spelling error could cause an editor to doubt your reliability and reject your story.

A news release may be prepared on either letterhead or standard typing paper. Ideally it should be limited to one page. If you must, however, use more than one sheet, the word *MORE* should be typed in the lower right corner of every page but the last, and all pages should be numbered successively in the upper right corner. The end of the release should be indicated with one of the following symbols:

```
-xxx-
000
# # #
-30-
```

The heading for a news release must include a release date:

FOR RELEASE
February 2, 19--

FOR RELEASE AFTER
4 P.M., February 1, 19--

FOR IMMEDIATE RELEASE

Also in the heading, if letterhead is not used, should be the company name and address as well as the telephone numbers of people whom an editor could contact for additional information. Following the heading you may either type a tentative title or leave an inch of white space for an editor to insert a title of her own.

The body of the news release should be double spaced; paragraphs should be indented five spaces. Margins of at least one inch should be left all around for copyeditors' comments. If photographs are enclosed with the release, they should be clearly labeled with a description of the event and the names of any people depicted.

Finally, the release should be addressed to The Editor, if sent to a newspaper, or to The News Director, if sent to a radio or television station. Of course, use the person's name if you know it. The envelope should bear the words: NEWS RELEASE ENCLOSED.

NEWS RELEASE

National Organization of Retired Persons
Fort Worth, Texas 76111
Zenaida Plonov, Publicity Director
(804) 771-1227

Marcia Lowe
The Editor
Fort Worth Gazette
(804) 771-2235

FOR RELEASE AFTER   4/4/--
3 P.M., April 7, 19--

ALVIN BANKS NAMED RETIRED PERSON OF THE YEAR

Fort Worth, April 7, 19--. Alvin Banks, outgoing president of
the Fort Worth Chapter of the National Organization of Retired
Persons, was named "Retired Person of the Year" at a luncheon in
his honor on April 7.

During his two years in office, Mr. Banks, the retired owner and
manager of Banks Building and Supply Company, helped the Fort
Worth Chapter grow from 53 members to its present high of 175
members. He instituted a number of the organization's current programs, including a part-time job placement service and a guest
lecture series.

Mr. Banks will be succeeded as president by Mrs. Beatrice
Toller, a retired buyer for Grayson's Department Store.

The Fort Worth Chapter of the National Organization of Retired
Persons meets Wednesday evenings at 7 P.M. at the Presbyterian
Church on Humboldt Street. Meetings are open to the public and
all retired persons are welcome to join.

# # #

★ PRACTICE CORRESPONDENCE

For each of the following situations, prepare a publicity-minded news release.

A. As director of the accounting department of the Waterford Stores, send a news release to the company newsletter announcing the addition of a new member to your staff. Marlon Strong, a certified public accountant, earned his bachelor's degree at Brockton College, where he was president of the Young Accountants Club during his junior and senior years. Before coming to Waterford, he was a junior accountant with Moyer and Moyer, a private accounting firm. Quote yourself as praising Mr. Strong's background and expertise and welcoming him to the company.

B. On Saturday, July 31, at 11 A.M., the Paperback Power Bookstore at 777 Main Street, Little Falls, New Jersey, will host an autograph session for Lillian Lockhart, author of the current bestseller, *The Office Worker's Weekday Diet Book.* The book, published by Knoll Books at $13.95, was described in the *New York Times* as "a valuable, must-read book for anyone who works in an office." Ms. Lockhart, a registered nutritionist, is also author of *Eat and Run: A Diet for Joggers,* among other books. Louis Putnam, owner of Paperback Power, has said that Ms. Lockhart's appearance at the store will be the first of a series of autographing events. Prepare a news release for the *Little Falls Press* announcing the event.

C. The Reliable Drug Store, 120 Franklin Street, Roscoe, New York, has been serving the community for over twenty years. On Monday, May 3, will take place the grand opening of a Health Food Annex to be located in what used to be Fred's Barber Shop, just to the right of Reliable's main store, at 118 Franklin Street. According to Marjorie Mansfield, present owner and daughter of the founder of Reliable Drug, Hiram Mansfield, the expansion was prompted by widespread interest in health foods as well as by increasing demand for top-quality vitamins and minerals. Ms. Mansfield said, "We intend to offer to small-town residents the variety of a big-city health food store and plan to carry everything from powdered yeast and protein to frozen yogurt and dried fruit." Write a news release to be sent to the local radio station making the expansion sound as newsworthy as possible.

13.
BUSINESS REPORTS

Information plays a vital role in the business world, nowadays more than ever before. The latest advances in computers, information-processing systems, and telecommunications have in fact made information a commodity in itself and those who process information valued members of the business community.

The purpose of a *business report* is to convey essential information in an organized, useful format. And despite technological advances, the ability to accumulate data, organize facts, and compose a readable text remains a highly marketable skill.

A well-prepared business report will provide COMPLETE, ACCURATE information about an aspect of a company's operations. The subject of a report may vary from expenses to profits, production to sales, marketing trends to customer relations. The information provided by a report is often meant to influence decisions, to determine changes, improvements, or solutions to problems. Therefore, the report must also be CLEAR, CONCISE, and READABLE.

The *format* of a business report may vary, from a brief *informal report* intended for in-house use to a voluminous *formal report* intended for national public distribution. Some reports consist entirely of prose while others consist of statistics; and still other reports may employ a combination of prose, tables, charts, and graphs.

The *style* of a report depends upon the audience. An informal report to be read only by close associates may be worded personally; in such a report "I" or "we" is acceptable. A formal report, on the other hand, must be impersonal and expressed entirely in the third person. Note the difference:

Informal: I recommend that the spring campaign concentrate on newspaper and television advertising.

Formal: It is recommended that the spring campaign concentrate on newspaper and television advertising.

Informal: After discussing the matter with our department managers, we came up with the following information.

Formal: The following report is based upon information provided by the managers of the Accounting, Marketing, Personnel, and Advertising Departments.

Whether formal or informal, however, the wording of a report should be SIMPLE and DIRECT.

Business reports are frequently divided into five *types:*

1) A Record Report merely states facts, describing the status of a company or of a division of a company at a particular point in time.
2) A Progress Report also states facts, tracing developments that have occurred over a period of time.
3) A Statistical Report presents numerical data, usually in the form of charts, tables, and graphs.
4) An Investigative Report is based on a study or investigation of a particular situation or issue. Such a report presents the newly accumulated data; it may also analyze the data.
5) A Recommendation Report is an investigative report taken one step further, providing specific recommendations based on the information provided.

Finally, there are three important *rules* to keep in mind when preparing any business report:

1) Cite your sources. *Always* let your reader know where your information comes from so that it may be verified.
2) Date your report. Business is volatile; facts and situations change daily, if not hourly. Your information could become outdated very quickly.
3) *Always* keep a copy of your report for your own reference.

Informal Reports

The informal report is the most common form of business report. It is usually short, five pages or fewer, and is generally drafted in the form of a memo (Figure 13-1), or a variation of a memo. Sometimes, if sent to someone outside the company, the informal report may be written as a letter (Figure 13-2).

The tone and style of an informal report will vary according to the subject and audience. But whether friendly or impersonal, a report must always be worded with courtesy and tact.

An informal report must often be prepared quickly, requiring that information be gathered more casually and unscientifically than for a formal report. Nevertheless, no matter how minor the topic nor how short the time, any business report must be THOROUGH and FACTUAL.

The best approach to accumulating data is to begin by defining your *purpose.* If you can express precisely the reason for your report, you will know what information to look for.

Once your data is assembled, the second phase of report writing is *organization.* You must arrange your facts in a logical sequence that can be easily followed.

Finally, the nature of your data and your system of organization will determine your form of *presentation.* If your report calls for prose, organize your paragraphs:

First Paragraph: Present the main idea clearly and concisely.

Middle Paragraphs: Develop the main point with supporting details and information.

Final Paragraph: State your *objective* conclusion. If called for, your own comments and recommendations may be included at the end.

TO: Mr. Marvin Dawson

FROM: Jim Coates

DATE: February 7, 19--

SUBJECT: Report on Secretarial Staff Overtime for January

As you requested, I have computed the number of overtime hours worked by the secretaries of the various departments and the cost of that overtime to the company.

Department	Employee	Hourly Wage	Number of Times	Total Hours	Total Cost @ Time & a Half
Executive	Ann Rogers	$7.50	6	15	$168.75
	Wilma Toynbee	7.50	5	14	157.50
Marketing	Maribel Cruz	5.00	8	17	127.50
Accounting	Nicole Foire	5.00	8	18	135.00
Personnel	Judy Hecht	6.00	10	21	189.00
	TOTALS		37	85	$777.75

The cost of hiring a clerical assistant for 35 hours a week at $4.25 an hour would be $148.75, or $595.00 and 140 hours a month. This would save the company approximately $182.75 yet provide an additional 55 clerical hours.

JC

Figure 13-1

INFORMAL REPORT (MEMO)

In a short, informal report, it is often a good idea to *itemize* your data. This may simply mean numbering your paragraphs. Or it may mean arranging tables of statistics. However you do it, itemization makes a report seem more organized and easier to read.

INTERNATIONAL INDUSTRIES, INC.
3000 Avenue of the Americas
New York, New York 10019

Dear Shareholder:

Subject: Third Quarter 1982 Report

Third-quarter earnings continued at record levels due to a significant increase in International's petroleum operations. Earnings for the first nine months of 1982 exceeded last year's full-year results.

International Industries' third-quarter income from continuing operations was $42,351,000 or $1.25 per common share, a 40% increase over the income of $30,330,000 or 89 cents per common share for the same period last year.

Operating income for International's petroleum operations increased 53% over the third quarter of last year, contributing over 79% of International's income.

As a result of depressed conditions in the automotive and railroad markets, International's earnings from fabricated metals products continued to decline. International Chemicals' overall quarterly earnings declined although full-year income from International Chemicals should be substantially above last year's levels.

International Industries is a leading manufacturer of petroleum equipment and services, metal products, and chemicals, with annual sales of $2 billion.

Laura M. Carson
Chairperson and Chief Executive Officer

Wayne G. Wagner
President and Chief Operating Officer

November 10, 1982

Figure 13-2

INFORMAL REPORT (LETTER)

INTERNATIONAL INDUSTRIES, INC.
Consolidated Statement of Income (Unaudited)
(In thousands, except per share)

	For the three months ended September 30	
	1982	1981
Revenues:		
Net sales	$517,858	$454,866
Income from investments in other companies	8,729	4,046
Other income (loss), net	2,599	990
Total revenues	$529,186	$459,902
Costs and expenses:		
Cost of goods sold	$339,851	$303,893
Selling, general & administrative	111,384	91,597
Interest	9,456	13,001
Minority interest	1,600	705
Total costs and expenses	$462,291	$409,196
Income before items shown below	$66,895	$50,706
Taxes on income	24,544	20,376
Income from continuing operations	$42,351	$30,330
Income from discontinued operations, net of income taxes	--	2,346
Income before cumulative effect of accounting change	$42,351	$ 32,676
Cumulative effect of accounting change	--	--
Net income	$42,351	$32,676
Income per share of common stock (*):		
Income from continuing operations	$1.25	$.89
Net income per share	$1.25	$.96

NOTE: (*) Income per share of common stock has been calculated after deduction for preferred stock dividend requirements of $.03 per share of common stock for the three months ended September 30.

Figure 13-2 (cont't)

INFORMAL REPORT (LETTER)

Formal Reports

A formal report (Figure 13-3) is not only longer, but more thorough than an informal report. It requires more extensive information gathering and is presented in a more stylized format. It is always presented objectively and relies on extensive details for documentation.

As for informal reports, begin preparing your formal report by pinpointing your topic. State the problem to be solved as precisely as you can. Then decide what information is needed to solve that problem and the techniques required to gather that information. Typical methods of information gathering include library research, surveys and interviews, and experimentation.

When your investigation is complete and your data is collected, you must organize and analyze the facts. Your interpretation may or may not be included in the final version of the report, but your own understanding and grasp of the material is essential before you begin to write.

When finished, your formal report will consist of the following parts:

1) TITLE PAGE: This page will include the title of the report as well as the name of the person who prepared the report, the name of the person for whom it was prepared, and the date on which it was completed. The title page, therefore, will contain a great deal of white space.

2) TABLE OF CONTENTS: This page will be outlined in advance, but it must be typed last. It consists of a list of all the headings and subheadings in the report and the number of the page on which each section begins.

3) INTRODUCTION: Unlike the introduction to a college term paper, this section is *not* an opening statement leading into your main topic. Rather, it is a statement of three specific facts:
   a. The purpose of your report (what the report demonstrates or proves);
   b. The scope of your report (what the report does and does *not* include);
   c. The method by which you gathered your information.

4) SUMMARY: This section is a concise statement of the main points covered in the report. Think of it as a courtesy for the busy executive who will not have enough time to read your entire report.

5) BODY: This is the essence of your report. It is the organized presentation of the data you have accumulated.

6) CONCLUSION: This is an *objective* statement of what the report has shown.

7) RECOMMENDATIONS: These should be made, when called for, *on the basis of the facts* included in the report. They should flow logically from the objective conclusion.

8) APPENDIX: This section consists of supplementary information, often in the form of graphs and charts, which does not fit into the body of the report but which is essential to substantiate the data.

9) BIBLIOGRAPHY: A listing of references used in preparing the report is required whenever printed material has been consulted. Entries are listed alphabetically by author's last name. Proper format varies from field to field, so you should consult a manual or style sheet. The following examples, though, will serve as general models:

Book: McLane, Helen J. Selecting, Developing and Retaining Women Executives. New York: Van Nostrand Reinhold, 1980.

Periodical: White, Kate. "Women and Success: How to Fight Your Fear of Trying." Mademoiselle, March 1981.

Figure 13-3
FORMAL REPORT

RECENT DEVELOPMENTS IN
OFFICE MACHINES

Prepared by Rachel Orloff
Prepared for Mr. Winston Chin
February 22, 19--

TITLE PAGE

Figure 13-3
FORMAL REPORT

TABLE OF CONTENTS

Figure 13-3
FORMAL REPORT

INTRODUCTION   3.

The purpose of this report is to examine the latest advances in office machines technology in order to determine what, if any, capital improvements should be made in the office equipment of the ANDMAR Corporation.

This report does not consider security systems or fire detection and control devices.

The information for this report was gathered from information supplied by the National Office Machines Dealers Association as well as from articles in several issues of Secretary's Press, Executive World, and Management Review.

SUMMARY

This report shows that, because of increasing emphasis on the use of very large-scale integrated circuits, major changes are anticipated in office machines during the next decade. These changes will primarily involve:

1. electronic typewriters with memory functions;
2. executive, as opposed to central, word-processing stations;
3. high-speed and intelligent copiers;
4. computers of increased speed, reliability, and memory capacity;
5. electronic printing calculators.

INT. ODUCTION AND SUMMARY

Figure 13-3
FORMAL REPORT

CONCLUSION AND RECOMMENDATIONS   4.

On the basis of the data in this report, it can be concluded that:

1. The installation of electronic typewriters and word-processing stations increases the productivity of secretaries and the efficiency of executives.
2. Medium-speed copiers maximize cost-effectiveness when used on a departmental basis.
3. Programmable electronic calculators function at a fraction of the cost of electronic adding machines.

From these conclusions, it is therefore recommended that:

1. An in-depth investigation of currently available electronic typewriters and word-processing systems be conducted to determine the cost and feasibility of installing such equipment.
2. A cost analysis be made to compare the copiers presently in use at ANDMAR versus alternatives now on the market.
3. The services of an electronic calculator system sales specialist be engaged to determine the equipment best suited to ANDMAR's particular application.

CONCLUSION AND RECOMMENDATIONS

When your report is complete and ready to be typed, keep in mind these guidelines for preparing the manuscript:

1) Use *standard manuscript form*—double space on one side of 8½" × 11" paper.
2) *Number every page*—except the title page—in the upper right-hand corner.
3) Leave lots of *white space*—allow ample margins as well as space between subtopics.
4) Use lots of *headings and subheadings*—make your report logical by giving headings of equal weight parallel wording; surround headings with white space.
5) Pay attention to *paragraphing*—try to keep your paragraphs more or less equal in length. (A paragraph of 15 lines should not be followed by one of 6 lines; on the other hand, paragraphs of 15 and 11 lines, although unequal, would not be too unbalanced.) Also, give each paragraph, like the report as a whole, a logical structure; start with a topic sentence and follow with supporting details.
6) Be sure to *footnote* information that you take from other sources—quotations should be followed by a raised number[1] and at the bottom of the page a notation made:

[1]Helen J. McLane, Selecting, Developing and Retaining Women Executives (New York: Van Nostrand Reinhold, 1980), pp. 71–73.

7) *Proofread* your report for errors in grammar, spelling, and punctuation.
8) Bind the finished manuscript securely.

★ **PRACTICE CORRESPONDENCE**

The following activities require that you prepare either a formal or an informal report. Be sure to employ an appropriate format.

A. Your employer has requested the latest closing prices of the following stocks (both preferred and common):

AT&T	General Motors
Eastman Kodak	IBM
Exxon	ITT

Consult a newspaper for the necessary information and present the data in an informal report.

B. A strike of the local transit workers union is anticipated in your community. In order to be prepared, your employer has asked you to investigate the cost of renting hotel rooms for the chief executives of the company. Contact a number of local hotels to find out their daily and weekly rates. Then present this information in an informal report. Include your recommendation for the most economical and convenient place to stay.

C. For a brochure to be put out by your local chamber of commerce, write a formal report describing at least half a dozen local restaurants. Consider such features as food quality and variety, prices, service, atmosphere, etc.

D. The Counseling Department of the Fort Worth Business Institute has been establishing transfer-of-credit agreements with other educational institutions in the region. As the school's assistant director of counseling, prepare a formal report detailing the course requirements for the major programs of study in your school. Include a brief description of the course content and the number of credits awarded for each course.

E. Imagine that you are the assistant casting director of a major film production company; the company is planning to produce a film version of a popular novel. Using a novel that you have recently read, write a formal report describing all the characters in the book and the actors to be considered for each role. Discuss at least two actors for each part.

LAST DETAILS

The final section of this book is intended to help you put some of the finishing touches on your correspondence. "A Glossary of Business Terms," though by no means exhaustive, will help you make certain that you are using specialized words in their proper business sense. "Catching Your Errors," a list of frequently used proofreaders' marks and commonly used correction symbols, will facilitate your proofreading your own work for errors as well as your comprehending corrections that others may make. And, finally, the list of both the traditional and the recently devised "ZIP Code" abbreviations of the states will serve as an easy reference when you address your envelope.

A GLOSSARY OF BUSINESS TERMS

account *n.* (1) a bookkeeping record of business transactions; (2) a customer or client.

accrue *v.* to accumulate, as interest.

affidavit *n.* a written oath.

amortization *n.* the gradual paying off of a debt at regular intervals.

annuity *n.* an investment that produces fixed yearly payments.

appraise *v.* to evaluate.

appreciate *v.* to increase in value.

arbitration *n.* settlement of a dispute through a third party.

arrears *n.* overdue debts.

assessment *n.* evaluation for the purpose of taxation.

asset *n.* something that is owned and of value.

audit (1) *n.* the checking of a business's financial records. (2) *v.* to check a business's financial records.

balance (1) *n.* the difference between debits and credits. (2) *v.* to reconcile the difference between debits and credits.

bankruptcy *n.* the legally declared state of being unable to pay debts.

beneficiary *n.* a person stipulated to receive benefits from a will, insurance policy, etc.

brokerage *n.* a business licensed to sell stocks and securities.

capital *n.* money or property owned or used by a business.

collateral *n.* property used as security for a loan.

compensation *n.* payment, reimbursement.

consignment *n.* shipment of goods to be paid for after resale.

corporation *n.* a business operating under a charter.

credit (1) *n.* the entry of a payment in an account. (2) *v.* to enter a payment in an account.

data processing *n.* the handling of information, especially statistical information, by computer.

debit (1) *n.* the entry of money owed in an account. (2) *v.* to enter money owed in an account.

debt *n.* money owed.

deficit *n.* a money shortage.

depreciate *v.* to decrease in value.

direct mail *n.* the sale of goods and services through the mail.

dividend *n.* a share of profits divided among the stockholders of a corporation.

endorse *v.* to sign the back of a check.

endowment *n.* money given, as a bequest.

equity *n.* the amount of money no longer owed on a purchase.

escrow *n.* written evidence of ownership held by a third party until specified conditions are met.

executor *n.* a person named to carry out someone else's will.

exemption *n.* money not subject to taxation.

expenditure *n.* an amount of money spent.

fiscal *adj.* financial.

flextime *n.* a system of flexible work hours.

forfeiture *n.* loss of property as a penalty for default or neglect.

franchise *n.* a special right to operate a business granted by the government or a corporation.

goodwill *n.* the value of a business's public image and reputation.

gross (1) *adj.* total, before deductions. (2) *v.* to earn a certain amount before deductions. (3) *n.* the total before deductions. (4) *n.* twelve dozen.

hardware *n.* the physical machinery of a computer.

information processing *n.* the "marriage" of data processing and word processing.

input *n.* data fed into a computer.

insurance *n.* the guarantee of compensation for a specified loss.

interest *n.* the fee charged for borrowing money.

inventory *n.* an itemized list of property or merchandise.

investment *n.* money put into a business or transaction to reap a profit.

invoice *n.* a list of goods shipped.

journal *n.* a written record of financial transactions.

lease (1) *n.* a contract for renting property. (2) *v.* to rent or let.

ledger *n.* a record book of debits and credits.

legacy *n.* money or property left in a will.

liability *n.* a debt or obligation.

lien *n.* a claim on property as security against a debt.

liquidity *n.* ability to turn assets into cash.

list price *n.* retail price as listed in a catalog.

margin *n.* difference between cost and selling price.

markup *n.* the percentage by which selling price is more than cost.

merger *n.* the combining of two or more companies into one.

middleman *n.* a businessperson who buys from a producer and resells at wholesale or retail in smaller quantities.

monetary *adj.* relating to money.

monopoly *n.* exclusive control of a commodity or service.

mortgage (1) *n.* the pledging of property as security for a loan. (2) *v.* to pledge property as security for a loan.

negotiable *adj.* transferable.

net (1) *n.* an amount left after deductions. (2) *v.* to clear as profit.

networking *n.* the establishing of business and professional contacts.

option *n.* the right to act on an offer at an established price within a limited time.

output *n.* data provided by a computer.

overhead *n.* the costs of running a business.

payable *adj.* owed.

personnel *n.* employees, staff.

petty cash *n.* money kept on hand for incidental purchases.

portfolio *n.* the various securities held by an investor.

power of attorney *n.* the written right to legally represent another person.

premium *n.* a payment, usually for an insurance policy.

productivity *n.* rate of yield or output.

proprietor *n.* owner.

prospectus *n.* a statement describing a business.

proxy *n.* authorization to vote for a stockholder at a meeting.

quorum *n.* the minimum number of members required to be present for the transaction of business at a meeting.

receivable *adj.* due.

remittance *n.* the sending of money in payment.

requisition *n.* a written request for supplies.

resume *n.* an outline of a job applicant's qualifications and experience.

rider *n.* an amendment to a document.

royalty *n.* a share of the profits from a book or invention paid to the author or patent holder.

security *n.* (1) funds or property held as a pledge of repayment; (2) a stock or bond.

shareholder *n.* one who owns shares of a corporation's stock.

software *n.* the data and programming of a computer.

solvent *adj.* able to pay debts.

stockholder *n.* one who owns stock in a company.

subsidy *n.* a monetary grant.

tariff *n.* a tax on imports or exports.

telecommunications *n.* high-speed communications via wire or microwave.

turnaround time *n.* time taken to complete a task.

trust *n.* a monopoly formed by a combination of corporations.

vita *n.* an outline of a job applicant's qualifications and experience, a resume.

word processing *n.* the handling of narrative information by computer.

CATCHING YOUR ERRORS

Proofreaders' Marks

ℒ	delete
ℒ͡	delete and close up
✓	less space
⌒	close up
∧	insert at this point (with insertion noted in margin)
#	space or more space
‖	straighten ends of lines
¶	begin a new paragraph
no ¶	no paragraph
ⓢⓟ	spell out
⊙	insert period
⋏	insert comma
⊙⋮	insert colon
⋏⋮	insert semicolon
⌄	insert apostrophe
⌄⌄	insert quotation marks
=/	insert hyphen
⊧	brackets
⊬	parentheses
⌢	transpose (with tr in the margin)
lc	lowercase (with slash through the letter in the text)
caps	put in <u>capitals</u> (drawn under letters in the text)
stet	restore crossed out words (with dots under words in the text)

Correction Symbols

SS	sentence structure or sense
frag	sentence fragment
CS	comma splice
r o	run-on sentence
dangl	dangling modifier
mm	misplaced modifier
//	faulty parallelism
sv /agr	faulty subject-verb agreement
t	incorrect verb tense
vf	incorrect verb form
pn /agr	faulty pronoun-noun agreement
case	incorrect pronoun case
ref	faulty pronoun reference
p	punctuation error
sp	spelling error
cap	use capitals
lc	use lowercase
awk	awkward wording
ww	wrong word
d	improper diction
l	faulty logic
coh	faulty coherence
dev	weak development

STATE ABBREVIATIONS

State	Traditional Abbreviation	Postal Service Abbreviation
Alabama	Ala.	AL
Alaska	—	AK
Arizona	Ariz.	AZ
Arkansas	Ark.	AR
California	Calif.	CA
Colorado	Colo.	CO
Connecticut	Conn.	CT
Delaware	Del.	DE
District of Columbia	D.C.	DC
Florida	Fla.	FL
Georgia	Ga.	GA
Hawaii	—	HI
Idaho	—	ID
Illinois	Ill.	IL
Indiana	Ind.	IN
Iowa	—	IA
Kansas	Kans.	KS
Kentucky	Ky.	KY
Louisiana	La.	LA
Maine	—	ME
Maryland	Md.	MD
Massachusetts	Mass.	MA
Michigan	Mich.	MI
Minnesota	Minn.	MN
Mississippi	Miss.	MS
Missouri	Mo.	MO
Montana	Mont.	MT
Nebraska	Nebr.	NE
Nevada	Nev.	NV
New Hampshire	N.H.	NH
New Jersey	N.J.	NJ
New Mexico	N.Mex.	NM
New York	N.Y.	NY
North Carolina	N.C.	NC
North Dakota	N.Dak.	ND
Ohio	—	OH
Oklahoma	Okla.	OK
Oregon	Oreg.	OR
Pennsylvania	Pa.	PA
Rhode Island	R.I.	RI
South Carolina	S.C.	SC
South Dakota	S.Dak.	SD
Tennessee	Tenn.	TN
Texas	Tex.	TX
Utah	—	UT

Vermont	Vt.	VT
Virginia	Va.	VA
Washington	Wash.	WA
West Virginia	W.Va.	WV
Wisconsin	Wis.	WI
Wyoming	Wyo.	WY

INDEX

BARRON'S POCKET GUIDES—

The handy, quick-reference tools that you can count on—no matter where you are!
All Books Only $3.95!! (Can. $5.50)

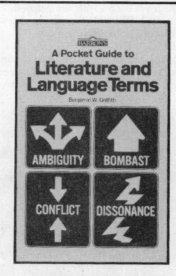

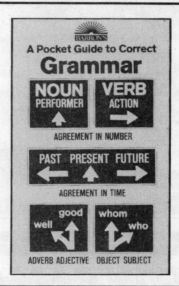

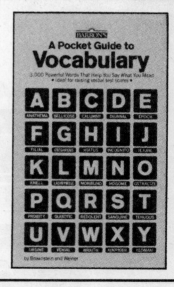

BARRON'S EDUCATIONAL SERIES

250 Wireless Boulevard
Hauppauge, New York 11788

In Canada: Georgetown Book Warehouse
34 Armstrong Avenue
Georgetown, Ont. L7G 4R9

Prices subject to change without notice. Books may be purchased at your bookstore, or by mail from Barron's. Enclose check or money order for total amount plus 10% for postage and handling (minimum charge $1.50). N.Y. residents add sales tax. All books are paperback editions.

$6.95

How to Write
Better Résumés

SECOND EDITION
by Adele Lewis

LET AN EXPERT GIVE YOU THE EDGE OVER THE COMPETITION! *STEP-BY-STEP GUIDELINES FOR RÉSUMÉS THAT GET RESULTS.*
- What you *must* include
- What you *may* include
- What you *must never* include

THE 5 BASIC RÉSUMÉ STYLES and the advantages of each—samples included. 120 MODEL RÉSUMÉS covering all levels from recent graduate to executive. NEARLY 300 JOB CATEGORIES. Plus: Worksheets to guide your résumé. Special résumés for special career needs.

Tips on writing cover letters—samples included. Complete job hunting strategies. Updated job outlook in selected fields and more! This book is guaranteed to help you
- Develop a dynamic professional résumé
- Get noticed by potential employers
- Open the door to a rewarding career

BARRON'S

BARRON'S

BUSINESS ENGLISH

A Complete Guide To Developing An Effective Business Writing Style

Essentials of grammar and usage: subject and verb • sentence structure • punctuation • capitalization • abbreviation • commonly confused words

Helpful guidelines for each category of business correspondence • Over 70 model letters showing correct format • Glossary of business terms

by Andrea B. Geffner

Dear Madam, Miss, Mrs., Ms....

Should I put a comma here or there...or...

To indent or not to indent, that is the question.

How do I write a nice nasty letter?

A proforma invoice! What's that?

Barron's Educational Series, Inc.

ISBN 0-8120-0669-0

$8.95

All prices are in U.S. dollars and subject to change without notice. At your local bookseller, or order direct adding 10% postage (minimum charge $1.50) plus applicable sales tax.

BARRON'S, 250 Wireless Boulevard, Hauppauge, N.Y. 11788